PILGRIMAGE TO

Dollywood

PILGRIMAGE TO

Dollywood

A COUNTRY MUSIC ROAD TRIP THROUGH TENNESSEE

Helen Morales

The University of Chicago Press

Chicago and London

Helen Morales moved from Cambridge, England, to Santa Barbara, California, where she is the Argyropoulos Professor of Hellenic Studies at the University of California, Santa Barbara.

The University of Chicago Press, Chicago 60637
The University of Chicago Press, Ltd., London
© 2014 by The University of Chicago
All rights reserved. Published 2014.
Printed in the United States of America

23 22 21 20 19 18 17 16 15 14   1 2 3 4 5

ISBN-13: 978-0-226-53652-1 (cloth)
ISBN-13: 978-0-226-12326-4 (e-book)
DOI: 10.7208/chicago/9780226123264.001.0001

Library of Congress Cataloging-in-Publication Data
Morales, Helen, author.
Pilgrimage to Dollywood : a country music road trip through
Tennessee / Helen Morales.
    pages cm — (Culture trails series)
Includes bibliographical references.
ISBN 978-0-226-53652-1 (cloth : alkaline paper) —
ISBN 978-0-226-12326-4 (e-book) 1. Parton, Dolly—Homes and
haunts. 2. Country musicians—Homes and haunts. 3. Musical land-
marks—Tennessee. 4. Tennessee—Description and travel. 5. Country
music fans—Travel. I. Title. II. Series: Culture trails.
ML420.P28M67 2014
781.64209768—dc23   2013044864

Contents

PILGRIMAGE TO

Dollywood

1

Caviar and Fish Sticks

In the early evening of May 7, 2010, I found myself jostling in a scrum of fevered adults and children lining the Parkway, the main road that runs through the small city of Pigeon Forge, in Sevier County, east Tennessee. We were there for the annual "Dolly Homecoming Parade," a carnival in honor of the city's most cherished celebrity and benefactor, the singer, movie actor, and businesswoman Dolly Parton, who was born and raised in Sevier County. This parade was particularly special: it marked the twenty-fifth anniversary of the opening of Dollywood, the local theme park partly owned by, and modeled around, the superstar and her life story. Most of us had been waiting for hours, the day suspended in anticipation of the few moments when we'd glimpse Dolly Parton. As she does every year, the singer would play grand marshal, heading the parade held in her name.

I had no idea what to expect from the parade or how to prepare for it, so I phoned Dollywood a few days ahead of my journey. The woman who took the call was kindly and proprietorial, as if this were *her* parade, *her* Dolly. She advised me to come at least six hours before the 6:00 p.m. start, and to mark my territory with a folding chair somewhere between traffic light 3 and traffic light 6 along the Parkway. "If you stay in one of the hotels along the route," she added, "you can visit the bathroom without losing your place." This was good advice and I took it, bringing with me on the flight a chair from Target (inexpensive and with an American flag design), and booking into the modest but friendly Shular Inn, situated toward the end of the parade route. It was an unprepossessing place to spend a day waiting. Outside the hotel on the narrow strip of grass between the building and the sidewalk was a massive sign in red, white, and blue tinsel declaring GOD BLESS AMERICA. The next building along was a shop that sold only things to do with Christmas. Traffic thundered along the Parkway, undeterred by the clusters of chairs that grew steadily along the roadside as the day wore on (fig. 1).

At midday, sitting low in my folding chair mesmerized by the stream of cars, I felt as ridiculous as I had always thought those families are who park by the side of highways and eat picnic lunches out of Tupperware. What was I doing, choking on exhaust fumes and slowly roasting in the oppressive Tennessee heat? There was one instant where I thought I must have succumbed to the swelter; I thought I saw Dolly Parton, a smudged and stretched Dolly Parton, leaning against the wall on the other side of the road, until I realized it was a transvestite *doppelganger*, dressed in a pale pink suit, with false bust and shiny platinum wig.

1. Staking out territory along the parade route

By 4:00 p.m., when the crowds arrived in earnest and people risked falling into the traffic to secure a spot, embarrassment and discomfort had turned into relief. We were an odd bunch. Some I talked to were locals, there to see their children who were in the parade as band players or majorettes. Others had made quite a journey. One couple came every year from Cleveland, Ohio. "We wouldn't miss it for the world," they beamed, as if we were standing on a beach in the Maldives, rather than a sidewalk packed with sweaty adults and fractious children. I spoke to Kate and Dan who had flown in from Perth, Australia. Like me, this was their first time at a Dolly Parade ("We've always wanted to see Dolly *for real*," said Dan). The warm bond of camaraderie shifted into tense competitiveness as the officious chuffing of a brass band announced the parade's arrival and we all jockeyed for a view (figs. 2 and 3).

It all then happened very quickly, like a film in fast-forward. Two proud boy scouts bearing a banner with the *Dollywood* logo, pinky-orange butterflies (butterflies are one of Dolly's chosen motifs) and the words

Welcome to the 25th Anniversary of
Dolly's Homecoming Parade
May 7, 2010
Proudly Presented by
The City of Pigeon Forge

Next, purple-clad children of the Sevier County High School Band, struggling by this stage of the march, and, behind them, the flash of an enormous silver and turquoise butterfly, antennae bobbing menacingly as if poised to swoop down and gobble up a flagging tuba player. The insect blocked the view of the silver truck, and then: there she was. Under an aquamarine parasol, perched on a white cube atop a three-tiered, silver-sashed wedding cake of a float sprinkled with silver, blue and purple butterflies, was Dolly Parton. I fought

2, 3. The Dolly Parade

to take in the shimmering lavender and silver lamé dress, the silver fairy wings, silver high heels, and blonde wig. *The blonde wig.* Unmistakably Dolly Parton, smiling and waving at the yelling throng. ("Dolly! Dolleeee!!!") She made eye contact just for a second, then turned to wave to the other side. ("Dolly! Over here!! Look at Me!!!") And then she was gone. Sevier County royalty: the Queen of Country Music.

4. A fleeting glimpse of Dolly on her float

This book is about my quest for Dolly Parton, my journey to learn more about her and her music, and the places important to both of them. It is not a biography: I have never met her (and would likely be gauche and clumsy if I did), nor would I feel comfortable prying into her private life. Calling her "Dolly" feels overly familiar, but as she is rarely referred to in the press as "Ms. Parton" or "Mrs. Dean," I am going to follow popular convention. My interest is partly intellectual. More than a performer, Dolly Parton is a cultural phenomenon. As an artist who "crossed over" into pop music, she changed what was possible in country music. She is a prolific songwriter, the largest employer in Sevier County, and creator of a theme park to herself; all of this invites analysis. However, this is also very much a personal project. This is not a book written from the Olympian heights of an objective observer: I confess up front that I love Dolly Parton and her music and have ever since I saw her in the movie 9 to 5, when I was eleven years old.

I had planned for the journey to start in Memphis, with a visit to one of the most celebrated modern pilgrimage sites: Graceland, the former home of the late Elvis Presley. The paths of Elvis and Dolly intersect (or fail to) at significant moments in their lives. It is impossible to tell a narrative about country music without including Elvis, the star who, so one story goes, nearly caused the death of the genre. Moreover, I was keen to see how Dollywood, a celebrity site created with the input of a living star, compared to Graceland, a home turned into a memorial to a star after his death. From Memphis, I had mapped out a route by car to Nashville via Hurricane Mills. Nashville is the "city of music": home of the Grand Ole Opry, the star-making concert that has been broadcast on the radio since 1925; the Country Music Hall of Fame and Museum, which honors the elite in the business (Dolly Parton has been a member since 1999); and the city where Dolly Parton has both a home and a gift shop called Trinkets and Treasures.

Hurricane Mills lies roughly halfway between Memphis and Nashville. It is a town that consists of little other than buildings owned by Loretta Lynn, the country music singer-songwriter whose success foreshadowed that of Dolly Parton. At Hurricane Mills we were promised a tour of Loretta Lynn's house, a museum of her life and memorabilia, and something Americans call a "dude ranch." After Nashville, it would be a straight drive to Pigeon Forge to see the parade and explore Locust Ridge, where Dolly grew up, and to take in Dolly Parton's Dixie Stampede Dinner Attraction ("The Most Fun Place to Eat in the Smokies!") and—the climax of the journey—to see the Dolly Parade and visit Dollywood. That was the plan. And then the floods came.

May Day 2010 slammed middle and west Tennessee, along with south and west Kentucky and north Mississippi, with a wall of torrential rain that lasted the best part of a week. It was called a one-thousand-year flood, suitably biblical terminology given the flood's cataclysmic effects. The Cumberland River burst its banks and twenty-one people died. In Nashville, the Grand Ole Opry House and the complex that it was a part of, the Gaylord Opryland Resort and Convention Center, were devastated. The Gaylord Opryland Hotel was flooded by ten feet of water. On news footage it looked like a set from *The Poseidon Adventure*, with tables and chairs floating in half-submerged opulence. Photographs of the parking lot at the nearby Opry Mills Mall show one large expanse of water, punctuated at precise intervals by tufts of treetops breaking the surface, as if the city were signaling its distress into space using Morse code. The music, of course, still played on: Marty Stuart performed at the city's War Memorial Auditorium instead of the Opry. However, on May 4, president Barack Obama declared Nashville a major disaster area; by the end of the week, almost a third of Tennessee received the same status.

In the circumstances, it was impossible to make my journey that week. I briefly entertained the idea of sticking to my plans as I watched the catastrophe unfold on CNN. After all, a pilgrimage was supposed to be arduous: a test of the devotee's strength and determination. However, fantasies of "writer on Jet Ski rescues stranded family (and dog); all kept warm by singing 'Love Is Like a Butterfly,'" soon gave way to a more realistic assessment of the situation. It also occurred to me that, even though west Tennessee was less badly affected, given the forecast of more rain moving westward, the Dolly Parade might well be canceled or postponed. I telephoned Dollywood and was put straight through to the lady who had earlier advised me on preparation for the parade. She was not impressed by my question, and reassured me that "nothing will stop the Dolly Parade: Miss Dolly wouldn't allow it. If it rains on Miss Dolly's parade, folks will carry umbrellas." So, even though it was to spoil the romantic cliché of a pilgrimage as an unbroken and teleological journey, I resigned myself to changing my plans. I decided to do the parade on May 7 (flying in and out of Knoxville and staying overnight in Pigeon Forge), and then to return a month or so later and spend ten days doing the pilgrimage properly, from Graceland to Dollywood. This would prove to be a blessing in disguise. Not only did it make me more reflective about why I was doing the journey and what I wanted to gain from it, but it also saved me from what would have been in hindsight a major error: staying at the Heartbreak Hotel, rather than at the Peabody. I will be forever grateful to Angela, the wise cab driver who took me from Pigeon Forge to the Knoxville airport, for advice on where to stay in Memphis. But that is to get ahead of myself: at this point some background to the project might be useful.

I had wanted to visit Dollywood ever since I learned that such a place existed. I was fascinated by the audacity, the sheer outrageousness of an adventure park themed around Dolly Parton. I imagined (rightly as it would turn out) glitz and glamor, and all things Dolly. However, I had not acted on my desire to visit Dollywood, despite having the time and resources to do so. Often the formative journeys that we take require a sense of what the ancient Greeks called *kairos*, which means the right time, the opportune moment which must be taken advantage of for something special to happen. *Kairos* came for me in the summer of 2010.

The year before I had moved from Cambridge, England, to Santa Barbara, California. The move was a life-changing opportunity for me. I am a classicist by profession and was teaching and researching ancient Greek and Roman literature at the University of Cambridge. Tony, my partner of a decade, was living in Santa Barbara and working, also as a classicist, at USC in Los Angeles. We have a child, Athena, then nine years old, and the long-distance relationship had been tough on all of us. The offer of a position at the University of California, Santa Barbara, meant goodbye to being a Cambridge don and single parent, and hello to a united family. It was also a move away from the largely elite student body studying classics at Cambridge, to the more diverse student population created by the American liberal arts education. America was not, I thought at the time, an unfamiliar place. Previously I had lived for short periods in Arizona and in Washington, DC. I also have a Texan ex-husband, a kind and placid man whom I met when he was serving in the US army in Portogruaro, Italy, where I was teaching English as a foreign language. He introduced me to supermarkets where you do not have to pack your own groceries (as you usually do in England), to the chaos of Las Vegas and the quiet of the desert, to supersized sodas, and to pamphlets from the army base urging you to "wear your military eyebrows with pride." I thought of America as home away from home. However, in the ten months since our relocation to Santa Barbara I had not settled in well. Southern California is initially dazzling: dazzling sea, dazzling sun, and dazzling smiles. But beneath the beauty and the flash I found a lack of connection, as if all the energy here is used up maintaining the surfaces of things and there is not enough left for meaning, recognition, and intimacy. It was also a period marked by the economic crisis, furloughs, and university "restructuring." I was unexpectedly anxious and agitated, and rather lonely. In retrospect, I think that it was this growing sense of restlessness and unease that stung me to think seriously about taking the journey that had previously been only a fantasy.

Reflecting back on my life I realize that I have often had this feeling of not belonging. I suspect that everyone feels this sometimes, but not everyone looks to Dolly Parton for consolation. She is the poster girl for not fitting in but being fabulous anyway. My late father, a Greek Cypriot who immigrated to England as a teenager to work in restaurant kitchens and send money back to his family in Cyprus, also used to listen to Dolly Parton. "This is our music," he would say when "Jolene" came on the radio. When as a child I felt too large, too loud, and too Greek, with a fondness for wearing sparkly tops and rainbow leg warmers, I never felt that I would be too much for Dolly, who often quips that she is "flashier than a drag queen's Christmas tree." She has also said, "I've always been a freak and different, oddball even in my childhood and my own family, so I can relate to people who are struggling and trying to find their true identity. I do not sit in the seat of judgment. I love people for who they are." This attitude, together with her exuberant sense of style, is what has made Dolly Parton a gay icon, and it was through a couple of gay friends at university, who owned every album Dolly had made, that I really got to know and appreciate her music, as well as her persona. I loved my university days. I had brilliant teachers and inspiring friends, but Cambridge was initially a strange, and estranging, environment, for a girl from a seaside town whose father (by this time) ran a fish and chips shop. I would often feel, to quote the lyrics of Dolly Parton's song "Fish out of Water," like "they're caviar and you're fish sticks." (It was a while before someone explained to me that "fish sticks" is American for "fish fingers.") And now in California two decades later, despite a PhD, publications to my name, and a wonderful partner and daughter, here I was feeling like a bloody fish stick again. The time had come to make a pilgrimage to Dollywood.

Is *pilgrimage* an affected, pretentious term for the trip I was about to take, especially when referring to Dollywood, whose name manages both to parody Hollywood and to connote little girls' toys, a far cry from the gravitas of Lourdes or Santiago di Compostela? Is *pilgrimage* a fancy word for holiday, and *pilgrim* a gussied-up term for tourist? I was pushed to ask these questions as some of my friends greeted news of my trip with hilarity and derision, a snobbishness that I suspect would not have been provoked by my going to the annual Bayreuth opera festival, or even to the shrine of the Lady of Guadalupe. Indeed, I would soon discover that for many people, especially but not only academics, neither Dolly Parton nor theme parks have sufficient social status or highbrow connotations to make them worthy of attention. Conversely, those in the country music business are often hostile to analysis and comment by outsiders, at least to judge from the reviews in the music press of the relatively few academic books that have been written about country music. Whatever terms I used, I realized, I would have little cheerleading to send me off on my travels.

The academic answer to the question of whether or not this should be called a pilgrimage, and here I am boiling down a whole subdiscipline of anthropology and religious stud-ies called "pilgrimage studies," is that boundaries between pilgrimage and tourism cannot be firmly or fruitfully drawn. This view is summed up in a quotation from Victor and Edith Turner, writing in 1978, that has become something of a mantra in pilgrimage studies: "A tourist is half a pilgrim, if a pilgrim is half a tourist." It is not sufficient to propose that a pilgrimage is made for religious or spiritual reasons, whereas a holiday is made for the purposes of curiosity, relaxation, and enjoyment. Even when a journey is to an established site of religious importance, and made by a person with devout inten-tions, the argument goes, he or she often has mixed motiva-tions. A person may travel to St. Peter's in Rome for religious reasons, but also take in a visit to the Colosseum and enjoy a gelato by the Trevi fountain. Conversely, someone who travels to Rome for the primary purpose of shopping may pop into St. Peter's and be so moved by the wonder of the experience that they forget about their credit cards. This is demonstrated in one of our earliest accounts of religious pilgrimage. In the *Life of Melania the Younger* (date uncertain, but she lived from c. 341

CE to c. 410 CE), the devout Christian Melania describes her journeys to famous monks in terms of "visit[ing] the saints" and setting forth for "spiritual *emporia*," a spiritual shopping expedition.

The difficulties of differentiating between pilgrimage and tourism are well illustrated by the organization of the papal visit to the UK in September 2010. People wanting to participate in the events attended by Pope Benedict were not allowed to do so under their own steam. They had to contact their local parish and travel as part of a "pilgrim group" with an assigned "pilgrim leader." Certain events cost as much as twenty-five pounds (around forty US dollars) per ticket, justified by church officials "because the pilgrims would be 'journeying' to see the pope, just as ancient pilgrims did, and would be provided with a pilgrim pack" (*The Independent*, July 29, 2010). The pilgrim pack contained a yellow bag, *Magnificat* booklet, pilgrim papal-visit poncho (in case of rain), diocese lanyard, wristband and pen, ID button, snacks, and the official papal-visit CD with a welcome message from David Cameron and the British government, conveyed by Lord Patten of Barnes, as well as a track "featuring *Britain's Got Talent* finalist, Liam McNally." Those unsatisfied with the offerings in the pilgrim pack might be guided toward the shopping section of thepapalvisit.org .uk website, which reassures: "We have lots of products available. We have souvenirs like mugs, pin badges, bookmarks, fridge magnets and key rings—all beautifully adorned with the Papal Cross Keys logo and Newman motto 'Heart Speaks Unto Heart.' For that personal touch, you can even customize the Papal Visit mugs and T-shirts with the name of your local parish."

The scholarly inclination to reject purist demarcations of pilgrimage and tourism must be correct and was borne out by my own travel arrangements. I was taking my partner Tony and daughter Athena with me, and the journey was not a special one for them in the same way as it was for me. I would

like to report that my family was accompanying me because
they too recognized the fabulousness of Dolly Parton, but this
would be a lie. Tony had little sense of Dolly Parton. He has
eclectic musical tastes, including classical music and opera,
and also the Rolling Stones, the Beatles, and Sheryl Crow,
but no country music. A keen traveler who has lived for long
periods of his life in Australia and North America, as well as
his native England, Tony is more easily attuned to cultural
differences than I am, and has had no problems acclimatiz-
ing to Southern California. His agenda was both to explore
Tennessee and to find out more about Dolly Parton, given
her importance to me. This was a relief because (and this is
an embarrassing confession) I needed Tony to do the driving.
I am very much an Englishwoman abroad, not in a floaty
Merchant-Ivory sort of way, but in a never-learned-to-drive,
terrified-of-freeways sort of way. Getting myself to Pigeon
Forge for the Dolly Parade had been relatively simple: I had
taken a flight to Knoxville, via Denver, and then a cab (driven
rather alarmingly by a one-armed cab driver) from Knoxville
airport to Pigeon Forge. But I could not take cabs across the
entire state, so I was grateful for Tony's support.

Athena was also amenable to making the journey. I had
a stroke of luck when I was explaining to her where we were
going and why. I showed her a photograph of Dolly Parton and
she got it into her head that we were going to see the character
Aunt Dolly (played by Parton) from the Disney Channel's *Hannah Montana*. I suspect she thought we might also see Miley
Cyrus, the teenage star of that show; it was expedient not to
disabuse her of this notion.

For me, in contrast, it was important that the journey have
certain elements to it that would make it different from a holiday. I wanted to gain a deeper understanding of Dolly Parton's
songs by exploring the places that feature in them. I hoped
that these places would show me another America, a friendlier
and less alien America than the one I was experiencing in Cali-

fornia. I also desired, in some inchoate sense, to say thank you to Dolly Parton, for her music and for being inspirational, and to pay some kind of homage to her. For this, it was necessary for me to invest the travel with a certain intensity and atmosphere, call it "sacrality" if you will, with which I would not invest a camping trip in Yosemite, or a visit to Alcatraz. Moreover, even though I was aware that the metaphor of pilgrimage as a life-changing journey is banal, I wanted to experience something special, to be open to change, and perhaps even to stumble on the extraordinary. I took to humming the lyrics of one of Dolly's songs, "Travelin' Thru," which she wrote for the soundtrack to the movie *Transamerica*, and which earned her a second Academy Award nomination (the first was for the song "9 to 5"):

Like the poor wayfaring stranger that they speak about in song
I'm just a weary pilgrim trying to find what feels like home.

2

A Series of Cravings

It looks like the perfect road trip: Dolly Parton, blonde hair blowing in the wind, a perk of excitement next to Elvis, whose blue eyes are focused on the road ahead as they speed through the Tennessee countryside in a red Cadillac convertible (fig. 5). In fact, it is a digitally created fantasy, a video commercial for the state of Tennessee. Dolly has been inserted into a scene from Elvis Presley's 1967 film *Clambake*, in place of the original passenger, actress Shelley Fabares. In the commercial, Dolly enthuses, "I've played a lot of stages over the years, but there's one I never get tired of that's set for a great time day or night: Tennessee." The scene then cuts to shots of the state's greatest hits: the Smoky Mountains, Graceland, Chattanooga, the Grand Old Opry, and Dollywood, with a reassuringly authoritative male voice-over: "There's no end to the beauty, music, and adventure starring in Tennessee. For an unforgettable vacation or weekend getaway any time of the year, we've got the perfect setting for you." Then back to Dolly, who turns to Elvis and urges, "Let's pick it up a little bit honey: there's all kinds of things to do in Tennessee. But next time let's take the *pink* Cadillac!" (A reference, aficionados will know, to Elvis's much-loved 1955 Cadillac Fleetwood 60, still kept at Graceland and painted the shade of pink that used to be cool but is now indelibly associated with breast cancer).

Elvis and Dolly, one imagines, would have had a lot to talk

5. Dolly and Elvis—from a commercial by the Tennessee
Department of Tourist Development

about. Both of their fathers were sharecroppers (in Vernon
Presley's case, for a short period during the Great Depres-
sion), agricultural workers who did not own the land which
they farmed and had to give a share of the crop they produced
to the landowner: subsistence-level work at best. Elvis and
Dolly could have compared notes on growing up in Tennessee:
Elvis's family moved to Memphis from Tupelo, Mississippi,
when he was thirteen, and Dolly has had a home in Tennessee all her life. They might have discussed how they had both
pushed the boundaries of country music. Or perhaps they
would have laughed over their choices of roles in dubious
movies. *Harum Scarum* and *Rhinestone* were both panned by
critics (though I admit to a fondness for *Rhinestone*). Or they
might have confessed how nervous they were when they each
first set foot on the stage of the Grand Ole Opry. Between the
two of them, Elvis Presley and Dolly Parton divide up the
whole state: Elvis's territory is to the west, Dolly's to the east,
with Nashville, home of country music and where both stars'
careers were shaped, roughly in the middle. Elvis and Dolly,
the King and the Queen of Tennessee. However, they never did
talk to each other. The two never even met.

Perhaps they would have, had Elvis been able to sing Dolly Parton's song "I Will Always Love You," as he had planned to do in 1974, a year after Dolly wrote and first performed it. According to Dolly, she received a phone call from Colonel Tom Parker, Elvis's manager, on the morning of the scheduled recording. Parker demanded that she sign over to them 50 percent of the publishing royalties. Recalls Dolly, "I was really quiet. I said, 'Well, it's already been a hit (for me). I wrote it and I've already published it. And this is the stuff I'm leaving for my family, when I'm dead and gone. That money goes in for stuff for my brothers and sisters and nieces and nephews. So I can't give up half the publishing.' And he said, 'Well then, we can't record it.'" This story is testament to Dolly Parton's steeliness and sense of self-worth, as well as her huge sense of responsibility to support her family. "I cried all night," she said. "Other people were saying, 'You're nuts. It's Elvis Presley. I mean, hell, I'd give him all of it.' I said, 'I can't do that. Something in my heart says don't do that.' Her "heart" (or what others might call remarkable business savvy) was rewarded when Whitney Houston recorded the song in 1997 for the soundtrack to her film *The Bodyguard*. Whitney's version turned Dolly Parton's part-whispered rendition, in turn tremulous, melancholic, determined (said to have been written as a farewell tribute by Dolly to her singing partner, Porter Wagoner, when she left him to begin her solo career), into a masochistic power ballad, belted out in Whitney's incomparable voice. Whitney's recording is the biggest-selling single of all time by a female artist and has earned Dolly Parton over six million dollars, an amount that has increased since Whitney Houston's death in February 2012. Financially at least, Dolly was right not to concede to Elvis's manager all those years ago: "When Whitney's version came out, I made enough money to buy Graceland."

Perhaps Dolly and Elvis would have met had Elvis not died in 1977 at the age of forty-two, a year older than I was when

I made the journey to visit his house and grave. In the video commercial, the digitally manufactured interaction between the two is not quite in sync, as if acknowledging their failure to meet. Indeed, the commercial strikes me as poignant. It is a much older Dolly Parton in the Cadillac alongside Elvis, even though in real life she is eleven years younger than he would have been (he was born in January 1935, she in January 1946). In contrast to the clarity of Dolly's image, that of Elvis is grainy and dated. He is trapped forever as a celluloid ghost; she is, at the time of my writing (and, please god, long beyond) alive and touring. And so Dolly Parton's life has become an illustration of what Elvis Presley's might have been, and his premature death and sanctification a glimpse of what she has avoided.

Unsurprisingly, I did not arrive in Memphis in a Cadillac (of any color), with the wind blowing in my hair. I arrived in the late evening, after a flight from LAX sandwiched between Athena grunting and punching the air as she played Angry Birds on my cell phone, and Tony fretting about whether or not we had remembered to cancel our delivery of the *LA Times*. We had dashed to the airport after Athena's school "graduation and promotion" ceremony that morning. Liking the school in general, I was unprepared for the horror of three hours of platitudinous smugness that comprised "graduation and promotion." A handout that listed the names of the sixth graders who were to give farewell speeches had a quotation from J. K. Rowling on the back that gives a sense of the occasion: "It is our choices . . . that show who we truly are, far more than our abilities." I pondered this as the children filed up and collected their certificates. It may be appropriate advice for Dumbledore to give a trainee wizard, but it seemed less convincing from an educational institution with patchy algebra results. The speeches themselves were excruciating. The rule seemed to be for the child to take a metaphor and bash it repeatedly as he or she might a piñata. "I am a pebble in a stream, grateful for the smooth shaping of the waters of education," "I am a hiker at Yosemite, moving through rock falls and hard climbs to reach the summit," and so on. When one boy opened with "I am a sandwich" I thought I might explode. So we were tired and grumpy on our way to Memphis and *not* in the zone of calm preparedness that I daresay a good pilgrim, or even a decent tourist, should be.

Nor were we prepared for the suffocating blanket of heat that pressed upon us once the plane door had opened after landing. No guidebook's matter-of-fact declaration that Tennessee in the summer is hot and humid can do justice to the weight and airlessness of that June heat. A woman ahead of us stumbled as she disembarked when her hand slipped straight off the metal handrail, slick with moisture. Stunned and gasping, we fell into a cab to head to the hotel. It was a short ride, most of it alongside the great Mississippi River, glinting thickly, like liquid coal. There was an air of menace about the Mississippi in the moonlight, as if the river were already plotting the next wave of floods that would devastate the region the following summer.

As we were motoring along, Athena pointed out a bridge whose two arches were lit up like a Christmas tree decoration. "Dolly Parton," said the cab driver. "The Dolly Parton Bridge." I was a bit fazed by this, not having heard of any such bridge, and faintly suspicious that the desire to seek out Dolly had become contagious. The distinctive architecture, like a giant upside-down bra, suggested a likely (if crude) explanation for the name, and when I had got to the hotel I Googled "Dolly Parton Bridge" for confirmation. It turns out to be six lanes of Interstate 40 that cross the Mississippi between West Memphis in Arkansas and Memphis in Tennessee. Its real name is the Hernando de Soto Bridge, after the sixteenth-century Spanish explorer said to have been the first European recorded to have crossed the Mississippi. Perhaps it's because that's such a dull and clichéd narrative of how a landmark came to be named, as much as its resemblance to a schoolboy sketch of a bust, that locals call it the Dolly Parton Bridge. (*Guinness World Records*, however, apparently refuses to look at bridges in a smutty way and instead recognizes the Hernando de Soto Bridge for looking like the letter *M*: "the largest freestanding letter of the alphabet in the world"). There are, I was intrigued to discover, other "Dolly Parton" bridges. There's a recently built one in the Netherlands on the outskirts of Amsterdam and another in Mobile, Alabama (really the General W. K. Wilson Jr. Bridge) that implausibly has two red warning lights on top of its arches, like cherries on a rude cake. All of this is faintly ridiculous, but it did make me reflect on what it must be like to be reduced to your bust. To some people, at least, Dolly Parton is synonymous with hers. Dolly has been complicit in this association, making frequent quips like "I'm the only girl to have left the Smoky Mountains and taken them with her," and admitting "I made more jokes about them than anyone else I guess," and by having her breasts lifted with cosmetic surgery. One of her mottos is "If I see something saggin', baggin' or draggin', I'm gonna have it nipped, tucked or sucked." She calls this "keeping my cartoon up."

One problem with making oneself into a cartoon is that it is not always possible to keep control of the image that results. The light, self-deprecating humor with which Dolly talks about herself has become in others' hands leering misogyny, from the smutty song "Dolly Parton's Tits" by MacLean and MacLean, to the serious music journalism of Nick Tosches, who omits discussion of Dolly Parton from his exposé of the country music industry, *Country: Living Legends and Dying Metaphors in America's Biggest Music*, with the dismissive boast "The valley of the shadow of Dolly Parton's cleavage was bypassed completely." On occasion the equation of Dolly with breasts has verged on the grotesque. "Dolly the sheep" was the first mammal to be cloned from an adult cell, rather than an embryo. Scientists at the Roslin Institute near Edinburgh in

Scotland performed nuclear transfer: they replaced the nucleus of an egg cell with the nucleus from the parent cell, in this case from the cell of an udder. The resulting embryo was implanted into the womb of a third ewe, a surrogate, and in 1996 Dolly the sheep was born. The scientist who headed the team, Ian Wilmut, explained the name for the cloned animal: "Dolly is derived from a mammary gland cell and we couldn't think of a more impressive pair of glands than Dolly Parton's." (It may come as little surprise that the Roslin Institute was later accused by a female employee of being a "boy's club," where the women were referred to as "lumpy jumpers"). Dolly the sheep was euthanized when she was nine years old because she had developed lung disease and severe arthritis. However, before the animal's decline, Dolly Parton is said to have offered her namesake a permanent home in the grounds of Dollywood. Characteristically, she responded to crudeness with grace and good humor. However, I wonder how often Dolly feels like Doralee, the character with a similar build and name to hers in 9 to 5: The Musical, and to whom Dolly gave the lyrics: "You only see tits, but get this: there's a heart under there . . . well ol' Double-D Doralee's gonna stick it to you."

We were staying at the Peabody Hotel on Union Street, near the Blues District of Memphis. I must confess that I had originally planned to book at the Elvis-themed Heartbreak Hotel, adjacent to Graceland. It sounded kitschy and witty and necessary to the Elvis experience. I had also wanted to be able to compare its themed spaces (like the Burnin' Love Suite) to the themed space of Dollywood. However I took the advice of Angela, the cab driver who drove me to Knoxville airport after the Dolly Parade, who said with some concern, "Not the Heartbreak Hotel. Unless you bring your own barbed wire. If you can afford it, stay at the Peabody." I knew it was essential for the success of my journey that Tony and Athena enjoy themselves. So I had booked hotels on a sliding scale of expense to gain early approval, from the Peabody in Memphis to a Best Western in Nashville, to the Bear Creek Inn (which was offering a "renovation package") in Gatlinburg.

Gliding through the doors of the Peabody to get from the sweltering outside to the cool inside is like stepping into another world. The main lobby is a grand sweep of splendor, from the pale marble floors to the glittering antique chandeliers that hang in the lobby itself and on the second floor, which overlooks the central space from balconies punctuated by thick marble colonnades. The more discrete glow of table lamps placed around the generous clusters of tables, sofas, and ornate chairs; the highly polished surfaces of marble, glass, and leather; all made the space light and luxurious. Dark cherrywood paneling on the front desk and saloon bar with its row of impeccably aligned bar stools—like a doll's house miniature, if doll's houses had bars—the dark wood of a grandfather clock and grand piano, scarlet accents among the furnishings, and walnut-and-coffee-colored swirls of the marble walls and pillars afforded a heft to balance the light. I felt like I'd walked onto the set of a production of Lorca's *The House of Bernarda Alba* that I once saw at the National Theatre in London and which provoked a full three minutes of applause before any of the actors on stage had even spoken. In fact the architecture of the hotel is Italianate, not Spanish, but like that theater set it transports its guests to a bygone age where plantation gentry might gather to play cards and sip smooth bourbon. The hotel literature calls it "the South's grand hotel," not Memphis's grand hotel or even Tennessee's grand hotel. Wearing jeans and a sweat-soaked T-shirt, I felt distinctly unlike a society matron as we checked in. I usually feel repelled by society grandeur. It smacks of British aristocracy and social inequity, all the Cambridge College "high table" feasts I had left behind. However, as we meandered through its cool spaces, pausing to listen to the gentle piano playing in the lobby, I found it hard not to succumb to the Peabody.

It is an institution with a strong sense of its own history

and endurance against the odds. The hotel opened on this site in 1925 (two years after the original Peabody, on a different site, had closed down), but its fortunes have fluctuated. In 1968 Martin Luther King Jr. was assassinated in a motel less than a mile south of the Peabody, and one cannot help wondering whether he would have been so easy a target had he been able to stay at the grander establishment. The murder and the riots that followed accelerated the desertion of the downtown area by white families and businesses, and the hotel was shut down. Purchased again in 1971, and after a reputed twenty-five-million-dollar makeover, the Peabody stands proud once more, a symbol of the urban renewal in Memphis that the hotel's reopening has helped stimulate.

The current hotel harks back to its earlier glory days. In 1935 the writer and historian David Cohn summed up the hotel's place in the American cultural imagination with the now much-quoted (not least by the hotel itself) description: "The Mississippi Delta begins in the lobby of the Peabody Hotel and ends on Catfish Row in Vicksburg. The Peabody is the Paris Ritz, the Cairo Shepherd's, the London Savoy of this section. If you stand near its fountain in the middle of the lobby . . . ultimately you will see everybody who is anybody in the Delta." It was not hard to take an imaginative leap in time to 1953 when the Peabody hosted the Humes High School prom, and an eighteen-year-old Elvis was said to have spent the evening drinking Cokes with his fourteen-year-old date, Regis Wilson (Elvis wore a blue tux, Regis a pink corsage) and not dancing to the band because, he said, he didn't know how. Such mirages are easy to conjure at the Peabody, which accommodates its ghosts with some panache.

However, the main reason it was difficult not to like the Peabody was its obsession with ducks. There are images of ducks everywhere: duck pictures on the walls, ducks inlaid in the marble floors, cakes in the shape of ducks served with napkins sporting a duck logo. The restaurant off the lobby is called

Dux, and the bar opposite, Mallards. Chic shops surrounding the lobby are devoted to duck merchandize (duck T-shirts, duck belts, duck candles, duck cutlery sets, duck chocolates, duck walking sticks) some of which, like the duck soaps, are also a feature in the hotel bedrooms. Twice a day there is a duck parade. In the morning, the ducks are led from their "palace" on the roof of the hotel into the elevator and down to the lobby where they waddle down a red carpet and into the fountain, in which they swim until the ritual is reversed in the late afternoon. Athena loved the hotel: it had become a live spot-the-duck competition, and she'd announce gleefully when she discovered another place where images of the birds were hidden ("They're on the shower curtain!"). The interior designers have gone to town with the zealousness of a teenage girl given permission to decorate her bedroom any way she wants. It is hard for an institution to be too *de haut en bas* when it is fixated with ducks.

We rose energetically next day at the crack of dawn and, having breakfasted and picked up the rented car, were soon navigating Elvis Presley Boulevard, an undistinguished four-lane highway lined with strip malls and used-car lots, on our way to Graceland. The soundtrack in my head was not "A Little More Conversation" or "Burning Love" (both favorites on my iPod) but Paul Simon's paean "Graceland." As in the song, my traveling companion was nine years old. As in the song, we believed that "we all would be received in Graceland." *Received* wasn't the right verb. *Herded* would be more accurate. Or maybe *processed*.

From the moment we entered the ticketing area (a larger, dirtier version than those at railway stations, plastered with advertisements for Elvis credit cards and Elvis tour packages), through waiting in line for the bus that would drive us to Graceland, and during the tour itself, we were jostled forward with a momentum that allowed little time for looking and reflecting. As a result, I experienced the place as a series of snapshots: images and snippets of information that were snatched into memory before the bark of a security guard (there are no tour guides) or the surge of other visitors at my back propelled me on. As the shuttle bus drove through the entrance to Graceland, across the street from the ticketing area, at some speed, and I was struggling to adjust the volume on the audio headsets we had been given, I only got a glimpse of the iconic wrought-iron gates to the property, fashioned like scrolls of music framed on either side by two stylized Elvises, playing guitars. We were not allowed to wander on the grass or given time to take in the neocolonial architecture of the mansion (fig. 6). The tour was to be of the downstairs of the house only "so as not to intrude upon Lisa Marie and the rest of the family's privacy." I suspect it is also to prevent visitors from checking out the bathroom where Elvis died, failing, according to his girlfriend at the time, to come back after a visit to the toilet. It would be hard for even the most respectful of Elvis admirers to look at the scene of this ignoble death without becoming prurient, and embarrassed.

The audio guide set the pace of the tour and invited us to focus on certain features (and therefore to miss others). This was too directed for me (and a bit cheesy, beginning with Elvis singing "Welcome to My World"), so I took my headset off and allowed myself simply to respond to what was there. However, this meant I couldn't point things out or discuss them with Tony and Athena because they were cocooned in their own audio-guide worlds. Graceland is much smaller than I had imagined (the official literature says 4,500 square feet), rather modest for a mansion, at least compared to the enormous stately homes dotted around the English countryside that I had been taken to as a child, like Chatsworth and Hardwick Hall. The living room set a tone of early seventies glamor: an expanse of white carpet, white sofa, white armchairs, white walls with mirrors inset, perhaps to make the space seem bigger. Then there was the gold: gold clock and lamp, gold edging

6. Graceland mansion

to the glass-topped table, gold fringes on the deep blue drapes.

Beyond a glass partition sporting two regal stained-glass peacocks in blues, yellows, and reds, we got a glimpse of the "music room" with its black grand piano. Elvis's funeral service was held in these two rooms; a light, happy, lived-in space for such a somber occasion. Moving briskly from there and past what used to be Elvis's parents' bedroom suite (his parents, grandmother, and aunt all lived at Graceland too), we viewed the kitchen, or what we could see of it from behind the velvet rope. It was only later, looking through books of photographs in the gift shop, that I could make out the avocado-green sink and dishwasher or the gold-colored refrigerator. At the time, craning to see what I could, all I managed was an impression of a nondescript 1970s kitchen with too busy a carpet and too much dark wood paneling for modern tastes. It was not specific enough to evoke Elvis, or a slice of Elvis's life. Instead the kitchen was imbued with a vague sadness that rooms frozen in time often have, an uninviting nostalgia for times past.

We then squeezed down to the basement via a staircase that felt like it had been imported from a small boat (how on earth did Elvis manage?), except that it was lined with mirrors (allowing a nine-year-old to create multiple refracted images of her beaming face). We peered into the TV room, aggressively decorated solely in black, yellow, and white, with mirrors in the bar area and tiny mirrors stitched into the rows of cushions, alternately yellow, white, yellow, white. We moved on to the pool room, with a kaleidoscope of colors and accordioned paper lining the walls and making the entire ceiling a giant circular fan, followed by the "jungle room," an extravagant den filled with carved wood furniture with animal and "African"-style totem-pole features, animal furs and feathers, hanging plants, and one wall comprising an indoor waterfall. Beyond these rooms we were taken to "special exhibit" areas with glass cases displaying items from Elvis's life: his gold records, his costumes and movie posters, his and his wife Priscilla's wedding outfits, toys from their daughter Lisa Marie's nursery, and other paraphernalia. The stiffness of the costumes on the headless manikins could hardly contrast more strongly with the dynamism and energy of the man who once wore them.

With all the pushing and jockeying for position I may well have missed quite a bit of what was on show, but I managed to take in enough to grasp that Graceland stages a strikingly sanitized version of Elvis's life story. There are no photos or television clips of him at Graceland in his later, troubled years, when his breathtaking beauty had turned into drug-fueled bloat. His living together before their marriage with the under-age Priscilla (what would now no doubt be called "grooming"), their subsequent divorce, and the political controversies about his music are either alluded to obliquely or passed over. One guidebook calls the biography staged at Graceland "a gentle fiction, a healing portrait of Elvis the way we wish to remember him." Perhaps. But in editing out the less idealized memories of a troubled and sometimes troublesome

Elvis, Graceland also edits out much that made him important, exceptional, and much loved.

It seems to be impossible to tell Elvis's life story without turning it into a morality play. Different narratives follow different moral trajectories. A selection of the most influential can be boiled down as follows. One is a straightforward version of the "from rags to riches" Horatio Alger myth. Musician Patti Scialfa spoke for many when she said, "Elvis to me is a symbol of tremendous promise and that kind of American hopefulness, where you can come from nowhere and having nothing and build yourself up and chase that American dream." Graceland promotes this account strongly, with this "Message from Lisa Marie Presley" underpinning the story told through the displays themselves: "There are many things about my father, Elvis Presley, that so many others and I can admire eternally. He rose from humble beginnings and when the realization of his dreams and aspirations exceeded all that he had imagined, it gave others hope—a new awareness of their own potential, whatever challenges they might be facing in life."

According to Elvis's daughter, his living the American dream makes him a paradigm, a role model who inspires others. The comedian and actor Eddie Murphy paints a more complex picture of the "rags to riches" biography of Elvis. This is in discussion with the film director Spike Lee in an interview in *Spin* magazine in 1990:

EDDIE MURPHY: I have a room with some Elvis pictures in it. I have a room with lots of pictures of Elvis. . . . You don't find him fascinating?

LEE: I wish he never died myself, so I wouldn't have to hear about him every single day.

MURPHY: You know what's interesting about Elvis? When he was getting ready to die, Elvis was broke, wearing big platforms and was like a joke in show business. It shows you how fucked up society is, 'cause in the movies they only want happy end-ings and shit. What happened is, when this man died, that was their happy ending. Elvis was their American dream, the poor boy that got rich and they hated him for it. And then he died and they turned him into this god form. And I think that's fascinating.

Another common way of telling Elvis's life is that he lived the American dream, but it was a dream available only to a white man, not a black one. This is how A. Whitney Brown presents it on *Saturday Night Live*: "And what *is* the American dream? . . . [M]aybe I can best express the American dream in a story. It's about a kid who grew up in Tupelo, Mississippi, in the early 1950s. He was a poor kid, but he had a rockin' guitar, some flashy clothes, and a wiggle in his hips—and he had that certain something, called 'talent.' Of course, he never made a nickel, because he was black, but two years later Elvis Presley made a fortune doing the same thing."

There's a more accusatory version of this narrative that has Elvis not only benefiting from racial discrimination, but also actively participating in it, stealing from black artists who came before him. This finds powerful expression in a short story by Alice Walker called "Nineteen Fifty-Five" in which a white male records a song written by a black female singer. The record makes him a star, but even though he sings the song over and over, on TV and in concerts, he does not understand it. This mystery eats away at him and he attempts, in vain, to extract illumination from the songwriter, giving her gifts, getting her to perform the song with him, and inviting her over to his house. In the end he dies, prematurely and in pain, fat, desperate, and alone, because he could not understand the music that made him famous, music that he had tried to own but that was not his. Walker's tale has a wider resonance, but is commonly read as a thinly veiled story of Elvis, whose song "Hound Dog" was first recorded (though not written by) the female blues singer Willie Mae Thornton. It gives imaginative voice to the recurrent criticism that Elvis did not deserve so much acclaim, because he and his promoters had raided black culture and repackaged it for mainstream success.

Since Elvis died, this idea has been taken and twisted so that Elvis has become, for some, a symbol of white supremacy. Cultural critic Erika Doss has discussed how during the 1950s fans appreciated Elvis's borrowings from black culture and his "personal commitment to racial and cultural integration." In contrast, she observes that many fans today "imagine an all-white Elvis that corresponds to their nostalgia for an American culture that never really existed, but which they fear is fading from national consciousness. . . . [M]any of today's fans have re-formed his image, and hence his historical meaning and memory, into one of reified whiteness." While we did not see any of the more extreme signs of the racist repackaging of Elvis that Doss observed when she visited Graceland—Confederate flags with Elvis's image in the middle, graffiti protesting Lisa Marie's then marriage to Michael Jackson—it was a striking feature of the tour that the only people on it were white. The security guards and gift shop assistants were largely black, but not one black person while we were there came to pay homage to Elvis or to visit the National Historic Landmark that was once his home.

Alice Walker's story also dramatizes another strand of the Elvis biography: that he failed to find happiness despite living the American dream. The story suggests that this came from the psychological damage done to the self when one person violates another. Others provide different explanations for Elvis's assumed unhappiness. He was a white-trash loser who was doomed to misery and committed suicide, according to Albert Goldman's scathing hatchet-job *Elvis* (1981), and equally nasty follow-up *Elvis: The Last 24 Hours* (1990). Or he was a talented star who fell victim to his dissolute lifestyle of alcohol, gluttony, and drugs: the cautionary tale found in the children's book that I'd bought for Athena, *Who Was Elvis*

Presley? by Geoff Edgers, John O'Brien, and Nancy Harrison, which might have been subtitled *Just Say "No," Kids!* Or perhaps a genius corrupted by America, as in the U2 song: "Elvis ate America before America ate him." Graceland suggests a diluted version of the latter when it suggests that Elvis was hurt by criticism. In Lisa Marie's words, "With his success came the accolades and respect he deserved. However, the fame also brought with it a harsh kind of scrutiny and judgment that no one should ever have to experience."

Was this a way of looking at the world that her father had bought into? One of the most fascinating artifacts at Graceland is a framed scroll, titled *The Penalty of Leadership*, a sermon written by Theodore F. MacManus and used in Cadillac advertisements since the 1920s. According to the Graceland official guidebook, in 1967 Elvis read one of these flyers and declared that, even though the sermon had been written years before he was born, the author could have been talking about his life story. The text laments the "reward and punishment" that leaders in every field must endure at the hands of their critics:

> Spiteful little voices in the domain of art were raised against our own Whistler as a mountebank, long after the big world had acclaimed him its greatest genius. Multitudes flocked to worship at the shrine of Wagner, while the little group of those whom he had dethroned and displaced argued angrily that he was no musician at all. . . . The leader is assailed because he is the leader, and the effort to equal him is merely added proof of that leadership. Failing to equal or excel, the follower seeks to depreciate and to destroy—but only confirms once more the superiority of that which he seeks to supplant.

In making the sparest of references to Elvis's "addiction to prescription drugs," but casting aspersions on his critics, the biography presented at Graceland implies that it was the naysayers who really killed Elvis.

It is part of Elvis's enduring fascination to so many that his life story is always more than that; it is also a take (celebratory, critical, twisted) upon the American dream. To think about Elvis is to think about America: its history and its values. As foreigner, I found this insight intellectually interesting as I staggered from the subterranean display rooms into the bright

7. Elvis's grave in the Meditation Garden at Graceland

sunlight and stifling heat of the outdoors. It was, however, emotionally unsatisfying. I wanted from Graceland (as I would from Dollywood) some intense emotional experience. I expected, I realized, to make a connection to the place and to the person, to be imbued with something *essentially them*. Maybe I would find it at Elvis's gravesite, in the Meditation Garden in the grounds of Graceland.

The Meditation Garden, as it is known, might have been a tranquil retreat when Elvis first designed it with antique Spanish stained-glass windows in the brick wall of a curved portico, a central pool spouting jets of water, and statues of angels punctuating the concrete walkways and flowerbeds. However, the excited squeals of other visitors and the relentless flashing of cameras made it hard to conjure any sense of spirituality. Tony, Athena, and I filed dutifully around, taking in the tributes of flowers (red hearts, yellow chrysanthemum teddy bears, and a large floral guitar) and the grave itself, between those of his grandmother Minnie Mae Presley, and his father Vernon Elvis Presley (fig. 7). Elvis had originally been laid to rest at the Forest Hill Cemetery in Memphis, but was relocated to his garden at Graceland after it became clear that his tomb was not safe from looters. The epitaph on his grave recognizes his talent, influence, and philanthropy, as well as the love of his family. It ends with the verses:

HE REVOLUTIONIZED THE FIELD OF MUSIC AND
RECEIVED ITS HIGHEST AWARDS.
HE BECAME A LIVING LEGEND IN HIS OWN TIME,
EARNING THE RESPECT AND LOVE OF MILLIONS.

GOD SAW THAT HE NEEDED SOME REST
AND CALLED HIM HOME TO BE WITH HIM.

WE MISS YOU, SON AND DADDY. I THANK GOD
THAT HE GAVE US YOU AS OUR SON.

Writing this out now, I feel quite moved, but at the time, reading it on the tomb illuminated in camera flashes, I did not. I went and stood by a railing and felt the weight of heat and anticlimax. Later I would mull over why I felt so little pathos, so little of anything. It was partly to do with having too high expectations. The very name of the place "Grace-land" promises something charismatic, something spiritual, yet it was named after the daughter of one Mr. Toof, the mansion's owner during the Civil War era, rather than any innate quality of the site itself. Had his daughter been called, say, Joan or Lucy rather than Grace, the effect would have been rather different.

My only previous experience of visiting the gravesite of a rock star was a chance visit to another gravesite of a legendary musician, Jim Morrison, the year before. This was on a similarly sweltering summer's day in the Cimetière du Père-Lachaise in Paris. I had been advised by a friend to visit the grave of Oscar Wilde and so found myself navigating what I can only describe, with no disrespect intended, as a miniature town of memorial, its stone roads lined with every conceivable kind of grave, some garish mausoleums, some stunning sepulchers. Wilde's ashes lie in a huge marble tomb designed by Jacob Epstein. It has what the guidebooks call a "modernist" male angel flying across the front, but which more precisely resembles fascist architecture, given the immense stiff expanse of the angel's wings and the grim starkness of the marble below. Wilde's whole tomb is covered in lipstick kisses, some glistening bright red or pink, others mere grease stains, long drained of color. It is staggeringly and wincingly inappropriate, violating both the style of the monument itself and the renowned aesthetic sensibilities of the man it honors. I shudder to think what Oscar Wilde would have thought of those who pressed their lips to his grave, and those who wrote graffiti in between the puckered imprints: "Au revoir, Oscar!," "Be ♥ Happy!"— and even, more enigmatically, "Sturm und Drang." I shudder even more to think of what he'd have made of the angel's castrated genitalia. Subsequent research suggested different reasons for the vandalism, that the genitalia were taken as a souvenir, or were gouged out in homophobic protest against the playwright, who during his lifetime had been incarcerated for "gross indecency," or what he called "the love that dare not speak its name." Either scenario seems grotesque, as does the "re-membering ceremony" by performance artist Leon Johnson, in which he is said to have restored the relief with a silver prosthesis (not in evidence when I saw the tomb in 2008).

The back of the tomb was also unexpected. There is no reference to Wilde's radical politics and life story, except obliquely, through the quotation of a verse from "The Ballad of Reading Gaol." His importance to theater is glossed over quickly ("Author of Salome and other beautiful works"). The emphasis instead falls on Wilde's prowess as a scholar, especially in ancient Greek and English literature. We are told that he won the Berkeley Gold Medal for Greek in 1874 at Trinity College Dublin, that he gained a first-class degree in Classical Moderations from Magdalen College, Oxford, in 1876, as well as a first-class in Literae Humaniores and the Newdigate Prize for English verse in 1878. Immediately after that the epitaph jumps to his death "fortified by the sacraments of the Church on 30 November 1900 at the Hotel D'Alsace, 13 Rue des Beaux Arts, Paris. RIP." Despite my loyalties to classics, this seems as odd as Elvis having his SAT scores detailed on his gravestone and his musical legacy reduced to "Singer of Hound Dog and other beautiful songs."

Trying to find my way out of the Paris cemetery, I was drawn to a stream of people gathering round another grave and went to investigate. It was the grave of Jim Morrison, lead singer of the Doors. Like Elvis, Morrison died prematurely, and his gravesite has long been the object of pilgrimage. All kinds of people were there, angling to see his grave and dedications (a guitar made of flowers, similar to that placed by Elvis's grave, and a bottle of whiskey), but standing aside from the crowd was a woman, middle-aged and rather ordinary-looking, except that she was sobbing as if her heart would burst. Seemingly unaware of the huddle of Italian youths nearby snickering and pointing, the woman was totally immersed in what can only be described as grief of the most abject kind. She sobbed and sobbed, her face a rictus of anguish. I have never forgotten this woman, and now, reflecting on the differences between my experience at Jim Morrison's grave and that of Elvis, I realize how much my responses were conditioned by the reactions of the other visitors. Had there been a sobbing woman by Elvis's grave, I would undoubtedly have been moved. I also realize that pilgrimage sites, despite best efforts, have little inherent sanctity. Whether or not they prove to be meaningful comes from a personal commitment to see them as such, and I had not made that commitment in Graceland.

"Horror vacui," muttered Tony. We were sitting in the cool of a diner back at Graceland Plaza, a row of shops and restaurants across the street from Graceland, and Athena was fully occupied eating an ice cream as big as her head.

"What?" I said.

"Horror vacui: dread of empty spaces." He gave me the look he reserves for slow students. "It's the phrase coined to describe a certain type of bad Renaissance painting that crams too much in. So much stuff. So much emphasis on the stuff. Excess without coherence. A series of cravings."

He was spot-on, but I didn't want to admit it. I took it personally that the first place we had visited was not a success and became stroppy. I argued with him that "excess" is a loaded term, and one with class bias. "Think of the Duchess of Windsor's motto that you can never be too rich or too thin. Members of privileged groups are always described in terms that suggest discipline and simplicity, whereas the lower classes are criticized for their lack of discipline and disarray. You're such a snob. Would you say King's College Chapel in Cambridge is excessive?"

"King's College Chapel has a coherent design. Graceland is all appetite, grasping. It hasn't worked out what it wants to mean, and its attempts at meaning are all out of control. So it ends up being facile bricolage."

"Can we buy souvenirs now?" said Athena, face covered in chocolate sauce.

"The thing is," said Tony as we mooched around the gift shop perusing an overwhelming array of Elvis-themed goods, "the reason musicians like Elvis mean so much to us is that their music becomes the soundtrack to our lives. 'Blue Moon' was playing at my first school dance. When I hear it I remember the feeling of sweaty anticipation I felt that night. Rock 'n' roll wasn't something you listened to. It was something you danced to. It's about first kisses, first crushes, the creation of memories."

I thought about this as I scanned the postcards. Several pictured a young, slim Elvis next to a recipe for one of his favorite foods. (The secret to peanut butter and banana sandwiches is, apparently, to melt butter in the skillet and brown the sandwiches on each side slowly.) It is true that one of the reasons Dolly Parton matters so much to me is that her songs have underscored special moments or heightened episodes in my life. Three snapshots come into mind. The first is of a weekend in July 1998. Newspaper journalists are laying siege outside my mother's house. One of my younger sisters has been caught cheating in her final exams at Oxford University and, because she is also president-elect of the Student Union on a "free education for all" ticket, the press is out for blood. My mother is not taking it well and insists that this scandal will devastate my brother, her youngest child. My brother is sitting at the computer, enthusiastically looking up famous alleged exam cheats and announcing them in thrilled tones: "Jeffrey Archer!" We open the newspapers. One has a photo of our mum's house, which in reality is a nice, three-bedroom Victorian terraced house. The photo has the adjoining houses edited out so that it looks like a mansion. The spin in the accompanying article is how the mighty have fallen. The photograph in the next paper makes the house look like a slum. The spin of this article is look what happens when you let Greek Cypriot immigrants into the country. "Richard Branson!" yells my brother. It is not a calm summer. My sister handles the situation with cool aplomb. My mother develops agoraphobia. I put "Light of a Clear Blue Morning" on my stereo and wear out the cassette tape, playing it over and over.

Snapshot two: my twenty-ninth birthday. I am out celebrating with three of my girlfriends, *Sex and the City*–style. We are merry with cocktails, and when "Jolene" comes on the pub jukebox, we join in singing, braying out the final syllable of the line: Jolene, Jolene, Jolene, *Jo-lee-ee-eene!* It is exhilarating, raucous fun. "Jolene" is one of the great women's anthems. This has little to do with the rest of the lyrics (which we sang with hilarity: "Please don't take my man!") and everything to do with the repetition of the name in crescendo. If a female equivalent is ever made to the scene in *Wayne's World* where the four dudes lip-sync to Queen's "Bohemian Rhapsody," then it ought involve four women singing and miming "Jolene." Perhaps with a chaser of "Baby, I'm Burning."

Snapshot three: I am younger and less caring of myself and others, and have been having an intimate relationship with a married professor, a charismatic narcissist to whom I am completely addicted despite the fact that the deceit frequently makes me sick; he is the erotic equivalent of a packet of Pringles. Eventually, I end the relationship (sort of, and not for the first time) but, while everything is still messy, he moves on to a pneumatic younger colleague and taunts me by describing their florid romps. No one comes out of this sorry tale well, not the narcissist, nor the colleague who, when the narcissist won't leave his wife, begins sleeping with the professor in the office opposite his (though here you have to admire her economy of effort), and certainly not me. I listen to "Shinola" and "The Salt in My Tears," whose pithy, angry lyrics articulate some of what I'm feeling in manageable sound bites ("You don't know love from Shinola" . . . "You ain't worth the salt in my tears").

A significant number of the songs that Dolly Parton has written or cowritten concern love affairs and cheating. Others, like "Shinola," are about the pain of loving the wrong man. Collectively they constitute an almanac of human misbehavior and misery. Broadly speaking, the cheating songs can be grouped into the following categories: I'm the "other woman" and it's thrilling but agony ("Cologne," "God Won't Get You"); I'm the cheating spouse and it's thrilling ("I Can't Be True"), but agony ("Loneliness Found Me"); you're cheating (or have cheated) on me and it's agony ("Dagger through the Heart," "Little Sparrow," "It's Sure Gonna Hurt," "Hey Lucky Lady," "I Wasted My Tears," "Made of Stone"); you cheated on me, it was agony, and now I'm leaving you ("The Salt in My Tears," "Blue Smoke," "If You Need Me," "Star of the Show," "The Camel's Heart," "Heartbreak Express"). There are different nuances to these themes, such as: you're not cheating on me, but you're thinking about it ("Barbara on Your Mind"); you're probably married, but I need loving ("It's All Wrong but It's All Right"); you cheated on me so I cheated on you in revenge ("Because One of Us Was Wrong"); we're having an affair and we ought to stop ("You and Me, Her and Him"); I want to have an affair, but would be found out ("He Would Know"); you're cheating on me but think I'm too stupid to notice ("Run That by Me One More Time"); there's no way you are going to take my man ("Best Woman Wins"); my man had an affair but it was my fault ("I Took Him For Granted"); my man is leaving me for his mistress, but she'll cheat on him ("She Never Met A Man [She Didn't Like]"); my man has married the woman who stole him and I intend to steal him back ("I Don't Want to Throw Rice . . . I want to throw rocks at her").

Something for everyone, and while the lyrics do not match

the poetic intensity of, say, Euripides, they have a direct-
ness that acknowledges suffering, together with a wit that
helps to alleviate it. A word of caution here: many of Dolly's
songs, especially those from her early years, celebrate what is
commonly called codependence. In these songs, the woman
loves too much, and is deeply and addictively enmeshed in
a relationship that causes her pain. If this sounds like you,
it may be best to listen to the following very sparingly: "As
Long as I Love" ("I hurt for you as long as I love you, and I'll
love you for as long as I live. . . . As long as I love you there'll
be pain") "Because I Love You" ("and any way you want me,
that's the way I am yours; love as strong as this lets you control
me"), "Dagger through the Heart" ("you've made hurtin' me
such an art; tossed around like a used box of crayons"), "Even
a Fool Would Let Go" ("neither one of us is free; still I want
to hold on"), "Hold Me" ("you know that you control me; I
depend on your lovin'"), "Holding on to You" ("you don't love
me, but I'm holdin' on to you"), "What Is It My Love?" ("these
moments of heaven are worth all this hell"), "Lost Forever in
Your Kiss" ("I've become a part of you, and I'll do anything you
want me to"), "More Than Their Share" ("I give an inch and
you take a mile, and you tell me to jump and I just ask how
high"), "Prime of Our Love" ("I have bowed to your needs like
a willow"), "Puppy Love" ("you're meaner to me than a mean
ol' crook, and I must confess I'm really hooked"), "Put It Off
until Tomorrow" ("leave me tomorrow, wo-wo, you've hurt
me enough today"), "The Only Way Out (Is to Walk over Me)"
("just to prove that I love you I'll crawl at your feet").

Songs package heightened emotions into manageable seg-
ments—three minutes of elation here, four minutes of anguish
there—and in doing so, they make the emotions seem manageable too. The best of Dolly's songs, like "Light of a Clear
Blue Morning," combine caring lyrics with the extraordinary
transcendent beauty of Dolly Parton's voice. Listening to Dolly
sing these songs is like administering to yourself an injection

of empathy, a little burst of love. So for me at least, Dolly Parton's music is more than just a soundtrack to life, but part of a tool kit for living (along with, and better for me than, vodka, chocolate, and occasional binge-viewing of *Project Runway*). Presumably, for others, Elvis Presley's music plays this role. What was missing at Graceland, ironically, was a real sense of the music. That's one reason we found it so joyless. In the shop where we browsed, a tinny version of Elvis singing *My Way* was playing. I suddenly felt faint and overwrought and did not argue when Athena presented me with "Elvis Pezley" to buy: a candy container that dispensed a powdery lozenge each time you lifted Elvis's head. Appetite followed by emptiness. Elvis Pezley seemed an appropriate authentication of our experience at Graceland.

We had planned to spend the whole day at Graceland, but had lost our desire to do the rest of the Platinum Tour, which involved looking around Elvis's airplanes and car collection. Instead we drove to that other great Memphis shrine, the National Civil Rights Museum, which is built in and around what used to be the Lorraine Motel, where Martin Luther King Jr. was assassinated on April 4, 1968. The modesty of the squat, two-story building, with its incongruously inviting retro motel sign, red-and-white wreath marking room 306, and somber black lettering marking the museum entrance, all conspire to create a memorial of unusual poignancy. In an inverse image to that of Graceland, Tony, Athena, and I were among the very few white visitors to the museum. It was hard to believe that Graceland and the National Civil Rights Museum were in the same city, let alone a few miles from each other. There is no discernible dialogue between the two shrines.

One of the most profoundly moving aspects of the museum for me was overhearing elderly black visitors discussing their own lived experiences of the events presented in the historical displays. It is a serious, detailed, and uncompromising museum, and it expanded what I knew about American

8. The Statue of Nathan Bedford Forrest in the
Nathan Bedford Forrest Park

history, the Civil War, the Jim Crow era, the Ku Klux Klan, and the civil rights movement, subjects that are likely to be familiar to Americans, but about which I had only a sketchy knowledge. In preparation for my trip I had read articles in the *Mountain Press*, Sevierville, one of the local newspapers for Dollywood. One piece reported that in 2004 the Ku Klux Klan had protested against "Gay Day" at Dollywood, an unofficial celebration of sexuality (which is to say that the park tolerates but does not help organize the event). I confess that when I read this I found it faintly preposterous. The Klan seemed to me an organization that belonged firmly in the past, ghoulish monsters consigned to history. And yet it still exists.

Here in Memphis, there is an insidious and mainstream refusal to put the terrorism of the Klan firmly in the past. This comes with the honoring of Nathan Bedford Forrest, whose biography is as contested as that of Elvis, but who is widely believed to have been the leader of the first chapter of the Klan formed in 1866, after the Confederacy lost the war. Tennessee was a divided state in the Civil War, Unionist in the East and Confederate in the West, suffering a mutual hostility that continued through and beyond the period of Reconstruction. Forrest was a Memphis slave trader, alderman, and Confederate general whose tomb and a statue honoring him form the centerpiece of Forrest Park, a large expanse of green approximately five miles west of the Civil Rights museum (fig. 8). The oppressive heat meant that when we visited the park we were the only people there apart from an old black man huddled on a bench clutching a brown paper bag. Beneath the figure of Forrest astride his horse and facing south (legend has it that this is because he said he would never turn his back on the South) is the epitaph

1904
Erected by his countrymen in honor
Of the military genius of
Lieutenant General Nathan Bedford Forrest
Confederate States Army
1861–1865

That evening Tony and I tried to explain to Athena why we found this disturbing. We were at B. B. King's Restaurant and Blues Club, eating fried catfish and fried green tomatoes. It is a well-known tourist spot a couple of blocks from the Peabody, and the formidable police presence in the tourist district dissuaded us from venturing further afield. I was outraged at there being a statue in honor of a Klan leader and was yelling about it above the loud blues music. Athena yelled back: "So it's not like the statues in England then, Mum? We have statues of nice people?" This punctured my self-righteousness. I found it hard to remember with precision any statues in public parks. I tend to blur them into types: general on horse, general not on horse. Tony, however, pointed out that Warrington, his hometown in the north of England, boasts a statue of Oliver Cromwell, the controversial political and military leader who was one of the signatories of King Charles I's death warrant in 1649 and was also responsible for the attempted genocide of Catholics in Scotland. Near a friend's house in Chatham, Kent, he remembered seeing a verdigris-mottled statue of Field Marshal Kitchener: "Lord Kitchener of Khartoum." The mustachioed figure on the "Your Country Needs You" posters, Kitchener was a ruthless conqueror of Sudan and, in the Second Boer War imprisoned Boer civilians in concentration camps. He was one of the first leaders ever to use a concentration camp. So, no, Athena, it cannot be said that England only has statues of nice people.

This discussion has not changed my discomfort about the public honoring of Nathan Bedford Forrest,* but it did give me a sharp reminder that I was experiencing Tennessee as an outsider. When you are foreign to a place, your vision is in some ways more acute, more curious, sensitive, and critical than it is when you're on home turf. Your distance helps defamiliarize your surroundings. This means that you see more clearly, but also that your filter is slightly askew. Things that remain in the background at home, like statues in parks, come to the foreground when abroad. Going on a pilgrimage means being a witness, but the questing outsider is both the most and the least well equipped for the job. It was important to me to do justice to Dolly Parton and to her home state, and this meant recognizing that while I may be fully initiated into the imaginary state envisaged in song and story, I was very much an interloper in the real Tennessee.

*In March 2013, when this book was already in press, the park was renamed Health Sciences Park. The Statue of Forrest remains.

3

Country Is as Country Does

LORETTA LYNN'S RANCH, HURRICANE MILLS

We had decided to break up the four-hour drive from Memphis to Nashville by stopping at Hurricane Mills, where Dolly Parton's fellow country star, Loretta Lynn, has a ranch and museum. Loretta Lynn is probably best known for her hit song, autobiography, and film, all called *Coal Miner's Daughter*. Sissy Spacek won an Oscar for her portrayal of Lynn in the film, which tells of her early life and rise to stardom as a country singer. Loretta was the second of eight children (one of whom went on to become the country singer Crystal Gayle) born into poverty in rural Kentucky. She got married at thirteen, or thereabouts (her exact age has proved controversial) to Oliver "Doolittle" Lynn, had four of their six children before she was nineteen, and became a grandmother by the age of twenty-nine. Musically, she broke new ground with songs that told about life from a woman's perspective and without idealizing hardship.

I had only a hazy knowledge of Loretta Lynn's life and work, above and beyond the album that she made with Dolly Parton and Tammy Wynette, *Honky Tonk Angels* (1993), and was a bit anxious about what Tony and Athena would make of the advertised "Dude Ranch" and "Coal Miner's Daughter Museum," especially after the disappointment of Graceland. We were all feeling a bit queasy from the heat and from having eaten vast amounts of fried food at B. B. King's the previous

evening (fried dill pickles, fried catfish, and fried green tomatoes) and, in my case, drinking too many cocktails. Perversely,
all we felt like eating the next morning was a fried breakfast,
a cholesterol-laden hair of the dog. So it was a sluggish trio
that jacked up the air conditioning and headed east on I-40 in
search of Hurricane Mills.

In her song "Tennessee Homesick Blues," Dolly Parton calls
Tennessee "the greenest state in the land of free." This is no
throwaway line. The green is relentless. So many trees thick-
eted either side of the freeway that it seemed in places less like
an interstate than a track through a forest. No doubt exacer-
bated by my hangover, after a half hour on the road the green
seemed aggressively intense, psychedelic like the color on a
television screen that needs adjusting. "Shrek would like this,"
mused Athena. We drove for two and a half hours straight,
and I mean straight: the freeway runs in a straight line directly
from Memphis to Hurricane Mills, apart from the last eight
miles or so where we turned off to the left along a more mean-
dering road. Hurricane Mills was originally founded in 1896 as
a place where grain, corn, and flour were processed and where
wool was carded. In 1974 Loretta and Doolittle Lynn bought a
twelve-hundred-acre plantation and went on to restore the old
mill and dam. It is said that Loretta Lynn now owns practically
the whole town, if *town* is not too grand a term for a population of approximately 700 people. There was little evidence of
business not associated with Loretta Lynn. We passed Cissie
Lynn's Country Store and Music Barn (Cissie Lynn is one of
her daughters), and then a restaurant with a sign in curly,
old-fashioned writing announcing Loretta Lynn's Kitchen.
Another turn and the environment changed abruptly and we
found ourselves on what was little more than a dirt path snak-
ing through grassland still waterlogged from the floods the
month before. Tony was convinced we had come the wrong
way and was not comforted by the sight of an iron bridge that
had collapsed into what we later learned was Hurricane Creek.

A month before our trip, Loretta Lynn wrote a new preface
for the reissue, in 2010, of her autobiography, originally published in 1976. In it she expresses relief that the flood damage
was not worse, and explains the appeal of her ranch: "So many
people come here. They camp out, you know. It's like their
home too. They have a good time because we're way out in the
country and that's what people want when they come to the
ranch—they want real country." By "real country" she means
not just location, but attitude, lifestyle, and music. These have
been fused together since the naming of country music, which
was originally called "hillbilly music" (hence Elvis's epithet,
"The Hillbilly Cat"). Legend has it that Ernest Tubb, one of the
pioneers of country music (and who was also, I was intrigued
to learn, the first artist to record Elvis's "Blue Christmas," occasional singing partner of Loretta Lynn, and inductee to the
Country Music Hall of Fame in the same year as Dolly Parton,
1999), single-handedly campaigned for the name of the genre
to be changed. Offended by the derogatory connotations of
the term *hillbilly*, Tubb proposed that his record label, Decca,
change their catalog label from *hillbilly* to *country*, explaining to producer Dave Kapp, "Most of us are from the country
originally—call it Country Music." When Kapp suggested
cowboy as an alternative, to trade on the popularity of western
music, Tubb suggested a compromise: "Country and Western
music." By the early 1950s, the new discourse had taken hold,
and country music (which in England is still better known as
country and western music) was born. This rebranding established the essential connection between the music, the land,
and a way of life.

It was not clear to me that Tony and Athena wanted "real
country" in any sense of the phrase. The sight of a muddy
campground and unappealing barn-like set of buildings
prompted Athena to say "When are we going?" and Tony to
think it. I marched them to a shady spot where I could see a
refreshment kiosk and ordered cold sodas and ice creams to

mollify them while I investigated the time of the next tour. The girl selling the sodas had to close the kiosk window completely between taking the order and handing over the snacks; it was the only way to protect her goods from the sweltering heat. I asked her if she'd met Loretta Lynn, whom I'd read lives somewhere on the estate. "No," she said shyly, "but it's one of my dreams to do so. People round here say she's a wonderful woman" and charged me two dollars apiece for the ice creams. Half an hour later, when I returned with tickets for the tour and a sense of the layout of the place I heard a couple complaining about the cost of the ice creams in loud, cross voices. I thought of the long lines outside the up-market frozen yogurt shop in downtown Santa Barbara where a small tub costs double that price.

Our tour guide was a large, affable man in cowboy hat and boots who spoke about Loretta Lynn with such affection and pride that the group rallied despite the inhuman temperature which made it hard to breathe. I think he introduced himself as Alan, though I only caught the long vowel sound. "We love Miss Dolly too around here," he assured me when he learned we were en route to Pigeon Forge. "Miss Dolly had it hard, like Miss Loretta." Our first stop illustrated just how hard Miss Loretta had indeed had it. It was a replica of Loretta Lynn's childhood home, a wooden cabin, with a small well out front and outhouse at the back. The original is still standing in Butcher Holler, Van Lear, Kentucky. According to Alan, Loretta Lynn's brother gives visitors who manage to find the place a personal tour. The replica cabin had been staged to conjure an eerie sense of presence. The radio at an angle on the side table in the living room, a (plastic) homemade fruit pie displayed on the dining room table, and a bowl of water for bathing set on the floor of the kitchen, made me feel that I had blundered into a family home whose inhabitants had just popped out, like Goldilocks and the three bears.

It was true to the description given in Lynn's autobiog-

9. The replica of the coal mine in which Loretta Lynn's father worked

raphy, with the walls papered with pages from the Sears,
Roebuck catalogue to stop the wind whistling through the
cracks. It was also like a set for the song "Coal Miner's Daughter," Alan's hearty if tuneless rendition of which animated the
exhibit. We saw pairs of children's shoes (in the summertime
they had to go barefoot, but in the wintertime they each had
a brand new pair, "money made by sellin' a hog") and the
washboard where Lynn's mother scrubbed clothes everyday:
"Why, I seen her fingers bleed; to complain there was no need;
she'd smile in Mommy's understanding way." From the replica
cabin we were guided into a simulated coal mine (fig. 9). The
mine had none of the *Little House on the Prairie* charm of the
cabin. We needed to crouch down as we inched along the paths
where we imagined the miners used to hammer out the coal.
The pressing claustrophobia of tunnel walls and close bodies,
the darkness and the heat, together with Alan's commentary
of how Loretta Lynn's father died of black lung from years of

inhaling the coal dust, created a genuinely moving and disturbing experience. In her autobiography, Lynn describes her father's work: "The seam of coal was only three feet high, and you can bet they didn't bother cutting the rock to give the men a place to stand up. That meant the miners had to crawl on their hands and knees and work on their sides or lying on their backs.... I feel real proud of Daddy for working in the mines. He kept his family alive by breaking his own body down. That's the only way to look at it." You believe her: there can have been nothing romantic about this way of life.

Lynn has described how their similar backgrounds have forged a special bond between her and Dolly Parton:

> I get along with all the women singers, but especially Dolly Parton, who was voted Female Vocalist of the Year in 1975. We're good friends because we talk the same hillbilly language. Dolly is from Tennessee, and when we get going, nobody can understand us.... Me and Dolly like to talk about the old days when we were poor. We can remember how the snow and rain used to blow through the cracks. One time Dolly asked me, "Remember when you had company coming, how you'd shoo the flies out the door with a towel, then slam the door real fast?" That's what it was like in those old cabins.

Moreover, both singers have fused together their life stories, music, and their public personas. Like "Coal Miners' Daughter," Dolly's songs "Coat of Many Colors" and "The Good Times (When Things Were Bad)" take inspiration from her own tough upbringing. Both singers communicate a real pride in where they have come from and in the love and ingenuity shown by their families in the grip of poverty. "When you're lookin' at me," sings Loretta, "you're lookin' at country." Dolly's uptempo echo in "Country Is as Country Does": "Country born and country bred, countrified and country-fed, a country heart and a country head, 'cause I'm country to the core."

Lynn and Parton (like Merle Haggard, George Jones, and
other country greats) suggest that hard-knock biographical
credentials are essential to becoming a country music singer.
Or as Hank Williams Sr. put it, "to sing like a hillbilly, you had
to have lived like a hillbilly. You had to have smelt a lot of mule
manure." This is the hard lesson learned by Sylvester Stallone's
New York cab driver character in the film *Rhinestone*: to become a country star and help Dolly Parton's barmaid character
escape her exploitative employer (bear with me here), he must
go to the country and live with rural farming folk. Country
music is renowned for being the music of the white working
classes, sung by and for hard-working, blue-collar men and
women. "Country" has become more than a music, lifestyle,
or persona; it is an identity in itself. Chely Wright, in her autobiography *Like Me: Confessions of a Heartland Country Singer*,
comments, "My folks declared that our family identity was
Country, just as some people identify themselves as Democrats
or Republicans."

Country music plays a key role in shaping "country" as an
identity, in repeatedly promoting certain values (family, God,
nation, being "for the low man on the totem pole" as Gretchen
Wilson puts it), but also challenges and nuances exactly what
is meant by being "country to the core." In her debut single
"Country Girl" in 2007, Rissi Palmer, one of the very few African American country artists, defines country ways that are
both traditional ("Come Sunday morning palms up in praise,"
"good home training") and also resistant to the strong connection between ideology and place that Loretta Lynn insists
upon ("It's a state of mind no matter where you're from; . . .
you don't have to be a Georgia peach from Savannah Beach
to say 'mmhmm'; . . . don't need no kin from West Virginia
to have it in ya; . . . show the world you're a country girl").
However, the model established by Loretta Lynn, Dolly Parton,
and others has proved a tenacious one, resulting in what I call
"biographical correctness," according to which the country

singer's upbringing and way of life are as important as his or her musical abilities. This can verge on parody. Reading *Coal Miner's Daughter* hot on the heels of Dolly Parton's autobiography, *Dolly: My Life and Other Unfinished Business*, and seeing the replica of Dolly Parton's childhood home at Dollywood a few days after seeing the replica of Loretta Lynn's childhood home, reduced these poignant individual experiences to formulas. It also set in motion a kind of competitive retro-penury that played out in my head like a version of Monty Python's "Four Yorkshiremen" sketch. "Seven siblings? Luxury! I had eleven siblings and we all had to share the same pee-sodden bed." "Bed? We dreamed of having a bed. We slept on the cold floor and lived on bread dipped in gravy made of brown flour and water." "Gravy? Luxury! I survived when I first moved to Nashville on hoarded ketchup packets!" (And so on until fade).

It can also be hard to distinguish between those who have genuinely earned their country spurs and those who can act the part. Since way back, country music has involved "fabricating authenticity," as the title of Richard Peterson's history of the genre would have it. When Loretta Lynn first played the Grand Ole Opry she shared the stage with Minnie Pearl, an uneducated mountain girl from Grinder's Switch whose loud catchphrase "How-dee!" and trademark straw hat with the label still hanging off it left no doubt that she was a figure of fun. Minnie Pearl was, however, not a real person but a character. She was created and acted by comedienne and singer Sarah Ophelia Colley Cannon, who by all accounts enjoyed a comfortable upbringing and graduated with a degree in theater studies from Ward-Belmont College, a prestigious women's seminary in Nashville. Lynn does not record how she felt about Cannon's caricature of a woman like her, but she does expose the double standards of the industry when she tells of how she was berated by a Grand Ole Opry official for being seen buying her clothes from a thrift store. Clearly some preferred the *idea* that country music was the province of the

working class to the reality of it. Nowadays some artists ignore
biographical correctness and do their own thing. Garth Brooks
did not let his being born into country music aristocracy and
graduating from university with a degree in advertising hold
him back. He is one of the most successful country artists of
all time, second only in solo album sales in the United States to
Elvis Presley. The reality is that a country singer no longer has
to have working-class origins, and, barring the odd exception
like Gretchen Wilson, most now do not.

This does not mean, however, that country music has
stopped being the music of the working classes in our cultural
imagination. This leads to the desire of some singers to adhere
to biographical correctness. Take this self-representation from
the website of Rhett Akins, one of the writers of the song "Kiss
My Country Ass," whose lyrics are an in-your-face affirmation
of what country means: " 'Cause I'm a front-porch sippin', guitar pickin', moonshine sippin', 'bacca juice spittin' country boy
from the woods." Alongside photographs of Akins in a cotton
field wearing a cowboy hat, perched on his pickup truck with
his guitar, and posing proudly over the carcass of a turkey, and
in another standing tall over a dead deer, is the following text:

> Some men are just born to be country singers. It has nothing
> to do with chart positions, signed deals or marketing plans. It
> has everything to do with a rowdy Friday night crowd singing
> along to a song you just wrote because they've immediately
> embraced the words. You've written about your life and theirs
> and the connection has nothing to do with music industry
> politics and everything to do with honest communication and
> gut reaction.
>
> Just ask Rhett Akins. The talented singer/songwriter re-
> leased a collection of songs, *People Like Me*, that reflect the life
> he leads on stage and off as a loving father, avid outdoorsman
> and a quintessential everyman who has much in common with
> the audiences he's been singing to for more than a decade.

A brilliant piece of marketing that tries to conflate, in the footsteps of Loretta Lynn, his biography, music, and professional persona. Unsurprising, perhaps, given that Akins studied business at the University of Georgia, a detail omitted from the version of his biography given here. Of course, there's nothing wrong in taking business studies and then becoming a country singer, but when performers exaggerate and distort their life stories to present themselves as "country boys from the woods," it at best lessens, and at worst mocks, the achievements of the real "country girls from the woods" Loretta Lynn and Dolly Parton.

I wonder if material success makes a country pose hard to sustain, whatever the singer's origins. Is an ass still a "country ass" if it's sitting on the front porch of a grand plantation home, rather than of a cabin in a holler? This question was brought into sharp relief when the tour group was taken straight from the simulated coal mine to Loretta Lynn's pre-Civil War plantation house, with its imposing façade of white Ionic columns. The Lynns bought the house and land in 1966: "To me it looked like the house 'Tara' in the movie *Gone with the Wind*," she wrote. "That was our dream house." The guidebook boasts through numbers ("a total of 14 rooms, eight fireplaces and 48 windows"), but we were more impressed by the real sense of its being a home that came across during our tour. Alan made details come alive for us: how Doolittle made the wagon wheel chandelier that hangs from the kitchen ceiling, and Loretta had stitched the orange burlap curtains. Others in the group were excited to see the kitchen where the Crisco commercials had been filmed; we did not then know what Crisco was, but kept quiet about it. The den was decorated with Native American curios. Loretta Lynn is proud of being part Cherokee Indian and has a museum of Native American artifacts on the site, as well as her own personal collection. Athena was captivated by the collections of salt and pepper shakers and Avon perfume bottles, neatly arranged in glass cabinets.

Unlike at Graceland, there was a strong sense of aesthetic coherence throughout, as well as a strong and happy presence throughout the home. The latter may be because the singer now lives next door to the plantation home, in another house obscured from view by a tall white fence. "She comes over often," said Alan. "She's home right now." I thought how strange it must be to live next door to the mansion that used to be your home and with a view of the replica of your childhood home. It must like having your whole life set before you, in domestic form. I would hate this unreservedly: I am relieved to have consigned to history most of the places I have lived, from the humble (the apartment we first lived in above the restaurant my father then worked in, or the student room infested with slugs) to the grand (the former nursing home that my parents bought with plans to renovate that were never realized, and that had something of *The Shining* about it). But it is clear that the plantation house is part and parcel of the American-dream narrative that began with the Butcher Holler cabin. The wealth she has earned in some way sanctifies the poverty she first experienced. Poverty is only ennobling, it is implied, if one has escaped it. The takeaway message is that Loretta Lynn is an example of what you can achieve if you are prepared to make sacrifices and work long and hard.

Lynn's ranch and museum present contradictory versions of her journey from poverty to wealth. One version is that of *The Cinderella Story*, the title of one of the souvenir booklets on sale in the museum bookshop. It sums up her career as follows: "Most of you already know about Loretta's Fairy Tale, Rags to Riches Legacy of how a Coal Miner's Daughter from Butcher Holler, Kentucky, rose to stardom and became a Living Legend in the Country Music Industry." The Prince Charming in this fairy tale is her husband, who was "the true strength behind her whole career and life." Lynn as a passive partner who owes it all to her late husband is a repeated motif, but one which denies her independence and innovation, at least in her song-writing. Another version is found in the Coal Miner's Daughter Museum, an extraordinary hybrid of junk shop and aircraft hangar ("18,000 square foot," says the statistic-enthusing brochure). The displays here emphasize how Lynn broke new ground in writing songs about women's lives from a woman's perspective. I confess that I was not able to experience the museum as calmly and carefully as I would have wanted. Tony and Athena were flagging in the heat, and after the tour had finished, Tony said that I had as long as it would take for them to eat another ice cream to see the museum. Charging around a museum like a game show contestant up against the clock is not the best way to see it, and my account is rather selective as a result.

The Coal Miner's Daughter Museum is one of the oddest museums I have ever visited. Perhaps the oddest thing about it is that half of the labels used to identify and describe the objects are typical professional display labels, but the other half are handwritten in felt-tipped pen on little white boards and signed "Loretta Lynn" or "LL." The poor legibility of some of these, coupled with elementary spelling errors ("to" repeatedly for "too"), adds to the impression of realism. It is as if a mad curator broke into the building during the night and defiantly stuck up her own thoughts about the exhibits. Imagine the improvements to the New York Met and the British Museum if this were to happen there. Out with solemn labels detailing sources and provenances; in with personal memories and anecdotes. By a cream Cadillac parked against a Grand Ole Opry backdrop was the notice: "This is my favorite car. It's a 1977 Cadillac. I wrote most of my songs in it while driving to and from town. I'm still gonna get it out and drive it. Loretta Lynn." In front of a display of her children's paraphernalia, including a cast from a broken arm and wedding dresses, is a note saying, "I made all my girls let me put these gowns in my museum. Jenny is my granddaughter. Patsy is going to bring me hers to." I wondered how long this notice had been here, and what level of frustration lies behind the public reminder to her daughter Patsy.

The sense of the personal continues through the strange juxtapositions between the objects on display. What links them are their importance to Loretta Lynn and her life. So a Christmas tree and a plastic Santa Claus wearing spectacles that Loretta had had in her home in 2002 appear next to a bedroom set that used to belong to Hank Williams Jr. The backdrop used on the TV show *Loretta Lynn and Friends* and the jeep that was used in the *Coal Miner's Daughter* film ("Tommy Lee put a dent in it"), are next to the Amateur National Motocross Championships paraphernalia. This seems particularly incongruous, but the annual motorcycle race is held at the ranch every August. Glitzy gowns and rows of awards sparkle. Turn the corner and there is a mock-up of the living room from Lynn's first Nashville home, with mismatched furniture, children's rag dolls, a wooden tricycle, and a bust of an Indian chief on a side table. Another replica: the Butcher Holler School where Lynn attended through eighth grade. It had a furnace with two wooden seats, blackboards and, a sentimental touch, five brown paper lunch bags.

The visual shifts from signs of present-day celebrity and wealth to reminders of an impoverished past suggest another response to the question I raised earlier: can one remain "country" when enjoying prosperity? The zigzagging of the museum displays from past to present and present to past respond, "Yes, but only if you never forget where you came from." This chimes with the lyrics of Dolly Parton's song "Country Is as Country Does":

> *I can live in a mansion or a double-wide,*
> *Eat sushi raw or my catfish fried.*
> . . .
> *Now I can drive a tractor or a Cadillac,*
> *I can fly first class or slum in the back,*

But I'll be the same ol' gal when I arrive.
I can wear denim or I can wear silk,
Drink champagne or chocolate milk,
Take the best or live with less,
'cause a country girl survives.

Like Loretta Lynn, who made Jack and Meg White of the White Stripes "chicken n' dumplings out at my house" when they came to visit her at her ranch (Jack White went on to produce her album *Van Lear Rose*), Dolly Parton presents a country identity of herself as unchanged by celebrity and wealth. This is emphasized in her autobiography ("Although I look like a drag queen's Christmas tree on the outside, I am at heart a simple country woman") and in her songs:

And what you see is what you get,
Nothing's ever changed me yet,
Nothing will, it's a pretty safe bet,
Cause I'm country through and through.

Dizzy from sensory overload, I sat near a huge silk flower arrangement ("Tanya Tucker made the beautiful flower arrangement just for me! I love you Tanya! LL") in front of a screen where you could watch tributes to Loretta Lynn, including one from Dolly, and clips of her being interviewed and receiving awards. One clip showed her being asked about "women's lib" and replying that she was not into feminism, but "I thought that if a woman does a man's job she should get paid for it." It was not a coincidence that Loretta Lynn's ascent to stardom occurred during the rise of the women's movement. The resentment and defiance in her song "The Pill," written in 1975, fifteen years after the contraceptive became widely available, still has the power to shock (and amuse) today. Lynn's "telling it like is," adds up to pithy social commentary, exposing the hardship of women's lives, and, in songs like "Rated X,"

the double standards for what was acceptable behavior for men
and for women. She always wrote from the woman's perspective, something she acknowledges in her autobiography: "In
the old days, country music was directed at the men—truck-
driving songs, easy women, cheating songs. I remember how
excited I got back in 1952, the first time I heard Kitty Wells sing
'It wasn't God who made Honky-Tonk Angels.' That was the
women's answer to that Hank Thompson record—See, Kitty
was presenting the woman's point of view, which is different
from the man's. And I always remembered that when I started
writing songs."

Throughout the museum there was a strong sense of other
country musicians forming a second family, with affectionate
tributes remembering Johnny and June Carter Cash, Lynn's
best friend Patsy Cline, Tanya Tucker, and many others,
among them a poster of Dolly Parton, signed by Dolly, with the
message "Loretta, I will always love you, *my little sister!!!* Thank
you for the inspiration. Dolly Parton 1993." Much country music scholarship and journalism concerns itself with charting
the divisions and antagonisms between artists and between
the different strands of country music that they are thought to
represent, but the picture of the industry presented in Lynn's
museum is one in which they are a big happy family. It is a
sentiment echoed in Dolly Parton's much-quoted opinion that
"saying somethin' about country music is like saying somethin'
about a brother or sister or my momma and daddy."

I encountered a different kind of family in the gift shop,
where the woman at the checkout told me that she had been
a friend of Loretta's for thirty-five years, and that "most of
the people who work here are friends or family." I regret now
being too reserved to put in a good word for the girl in the
refreshment kiosk keen to meet her employer. Instead I blundered apologetically to where Tony and Athena were expiring
from heat and impatience, and together we made it back to the
car and the relief of air conditioning. It took another hour and

a half to drive to Nashville, a journey undistinguished except for the unexpected signage along the freeway: "Fireworks Factory," followed by "Adult Store," and then "Freshwater Pearl Museum." I wondered whether any one person ever stops off to visit all three attractions. Once we had checked into the Best Western just off Interstate 40 (perfectly decent, despite the grotesque life-size mannequin of Elvis at the entrance to the bar), and staggered over the road for an excellent curry, it was all we could do to sprawl on our beds, eat duck-shaped Peabody chocolates, and channel surf. I caught the last half of *Coal Miner's Daughter* on CMT. I know that seems contrived, but it is true (and for all I know CMT might play *Coal Miner's Daughter* 24/7). We shared a childish thrill in spotting things in the movie that we had seen that very afternoon. I was struck again by Loretta Lynn's toughness and steely radicalism. There was no doubt that my trip to Hurricane Mills had given me a renewed admiration for her. But I also knew that I would never love her the way I love Dolly. I realized that one reason for this, and a big difference between the two singers, is that what is striking about Loretta's songs is her fatalism, and what is memorable about Dolly's is her optimism. I put "Better Get to Livin'" on my iPod and fell straight to sleep.

4

Music City, USA NASHVILLE

What's in a name? The guidebooks say that Nashville was
named after Francis Nash, a general in the Revolutionary
War, and that it was originally called Nashborough (founded
in 1779). Some may prefer a less worthy alternative history
in which the city was named after Simon Nash, a local eccentric who bribed people by handing out free whiskey: "A
man named Nash walked out with a bucket full of corn licker
and plenty of dippers and proposed that the town be named
Nashville" (*Herald*, December 24, 1909). The origins of the
city's nickname, "Music City, USA," are also uncertain. Some
say that it stems from a compliment by Queen Victoria who,
in 1866, heard a performance by the Fisk Jubilee Singers and
responded, "You must come from the music city." Others give
the credit to an announcer on WSM-AM (the radio station
that broadcasts the Grand Ole Opry) who used the name during a broadcast in 1950 and it caught on. "Music City" is Nashville's most famous epithet, but well before its musical renown
the city was celebrated for being a center of education with a
number of distinguished universities, and, accordingly, coined
a soubriquet that harked back to the ancient seat of classical
learning: "the Athens of the South."

Like its ancient twin, Nashville has a Parthenon, and,
despite my weakly suggesting over a bagel and coffee breakfast
that we should head straight to the Country Music Hall of
Fame, Tony and Athena insisted that the Parthenon would

be our first stop. "There'll be no twanging there," Tony muttered rebelliously, while Athena was excited about seeing the temple to "her" goddess. My daughter is named for the patron deity of ancient Athens, the Greek goddess of wisdom. I do not much go in for giving advice to prospective parents, but I will say this, that you could do worse than name your child after a mythological or religious figure commonly found in paintings and sculpture. It may be risking punishment for hubris down the line (for me when Athena turns out to be a witless egotist with a god complex) but it is worth it for the hours of fun (for them) and relaxation (for you) while they run around museums and galleries happily searching for images of their namesakes.

The Nashville Parthenon was built to represent the city of Nashville at the Tennessee Centennial Exposition in 1879, a six-month-long celebration of the state's incorporation into the union a hundred years earlier (fig. 10). The exposition was an ancestor of the modern theme park. It boasted buildings that represented Tennessee cities (e.g., a giant pyramid for Memphis, which had been named after the ancient Egyptian city), showcased state interests (e.g., agriculture, fine arts, and education), and introduced visitors to foreign attractions (Venice was recreated on Lake Watauga, with gondolas and the Rialto Bridge), as well as fairground rides and firework displays. The Nashville Parthenon functioned as the exposition's Fine Arts Building, with a large interior exhibition space for paintings and sculptures. As the exposition closed, the citizens of Nashville objected to the demolishing of the Parthenon along with the other buildings. The land surrounding it was landscaped into Nashville's first large public park, Centennial Park. The Parthenon was renovated using reinforced concrete, with quartz mixed into concrete aggregate to give the sparkling appearance of the Pentelic marble of the original. The work was completed in 1931. Contemporary accounts of its construction stressed that it was an "exact replica" of the Greek

10. The Nashville Parthenon, built to celebrate "the Athens of the South"

temple, built in the fifth century BCE and now surviving only in ruins and plundered fragments. However, one of its many differences, much appreciated by our heat-stricken party, is that it is not placed on top of an acropolis, but on the flat with only a few steps to climb and in lush green surroundings by Lake Watauga, a half-mile drive from our hotel.

Plato would have been greatly perturbed by the Nashville Parthenon. His philosophy turns repeatedly to the subject of copies, mimetic representations of originals. The problem for Plato would have been that, in several respects, the Nashville Parthenon does not, and, given the gaps in our knowledge, cannot, look exactly like the original Athenian temple. The sculptors of the pediments, Leopold and Belle Kinney Scholz, were meticulous in crafting them using casts of the Elgin Marbles, but as these survive only in fragments, the scenes of gods and goddesses on the Nashville pediments are imaginative reconstructions that fill in the gaps. Plato worried that

poor copies of things detracted from their originals, which
contained essential truths. The Nashville Parthenon, modeled
on a modern idea of an ancient temple to the patron goddess
of Athens, would in Plato's eyes have demeaned the original: a
blasphemous pretender. I realized that I had expected to find
the Nashville Parthenon a lesser monument than the Athenian
original (or my idea of the Athenian original), an interesting
example of late nineteenth-century neoclassical architecture,
perhaps, like so many banks and law courts. In this I was not
only being Platonic, valuing the original over the copy, I was
also wildly wrong.

The temple signals its gravitas through two sets of bronze
doors (weighing 7.5 tons each, we would later learn) designed
to make the visitor feel like an intruder into an inner sanctum.
A little way inside the cool interior stands a statue of Athena,
a terrifying blaze of gold and white, with massive blue eyes
staring from an impassive warrior face. The red mouth of a
screaming gorgon's head is the only punctuation of color to
the gold breastplate and robe. "Awesome" is so overused a
term that it now connotes its opposite, banality (I hear it said
most often when I grant a student a paper extension or an add
code), but the clichés of being awestruck are true: the hairs
on the back of my neck stood up; I almost wet myself; I was
rooted to the spot and stood there gape-mouthed. I am aware
that this sounds a touch overheated, but I have never been as
overwhelmed by the sight of anything as I was in the presence
of the Nashville Athena. She is colossal: at over forty-one
feet tall, this is the largest indoor statue in the world (fig. 11).
The original cult statue from Athens does not survive. The
Nashville statue is the original work of Alan LeQuire, whose
creation surpasses any ancient description or extant image
of a statue of Athena. The gilding and painting are crucial to
the statue's extraordinary impact and were done relatively
recently in 2002. This happened after the scenes had been shot
for the movie *Percy Jackson and the Lightning Thief* in which

11. My nine year old daughter Athena in the foreground gives some idea of the height of the magnificent statue of her namesake.

the teenage heroes battle a fire-breathing hydra after snatching a pearl from the then decidedly anemic statue's crown. The Greeks thought that the gods sometimes inhabited their cult statues, that the sculpture was both object and deity. The Nashville Athena gave me some understanding of this and of epiphany: the god made manifest on earth.

None of this can be experienced today at the ruins of the "real" Parthenon in Athens, a ruin overrun with tourists. The terms *replica* and *copy* as used in the museum literature and guidebooks are inadequate to account for the Nashville Parthenon. The monument may in some very limited ways be a replica of the imagined original, but it is also very much its own monument. Its impressiveness does not lie in likeness to something else, but in its very singular attributes. On a theoretical level, the Nashville Parthenon would support the challenge to Plato by the French philosopher Gilles Deleuze. Deleuze sought to reverse the hierarchy of original over copy when he argued for the independent power of the simulacrum, which in his use of the term means a version whose importance lies not in its resemblance to, but in its difference from, an existing image. ("Original" is now misleading, as a simulacrum is also, according to Deleuze, an original.) On a more mundane level, I mused, boy, haven't today's Greeks missed a trick? All of that scrapping with the British Museum over possession of the Parthenon marbles when they could have been building this instead.

I struck up a conversation with a security guard at the doors. I had read on the web that people came to worship the goddess Athena in the Nashville Parthenon. "I'm a librarian, a Hellenic Polytheist, a Traditional Wiccan, and an occultist," writes one blogger from Indiana, in a self-description that manages to make "librarian" sound sinister. "My family and I are planning a pilgrimage to the Nashville Parthenon on Saturday April 10, 2010. We'll be there at Noon EST until they close at 4:30 p.m. and we'd love to see some friendly faces from the Hellenic community there." I was skeptical about the reality of this kind of pilgrimage. The guard assured me that it happened, if not frequently. Every so often, she said, worshippers would come in robes and perform rituals with barley ("we don't allow much of that unless they make sure they clear up afterward"). I am inclined to find this a bit loopy. Modern goddess worship is invested in a romanticized and unfounded view of ancient religions, that goddess worship was matrifocal: sadly untrue. But I am also struck by the need many of us have, and the imaginative ways we seek to fulfill it, to be inspired, adoring, and bathed in light.

It is often pointed out, usually with much handwringing, that obsession with celebrities has become a modern religion. The similarities between religion and fandom are obvious: the adoration of a charismatic figure, the valuing of special places and objects associated with them, and the sense of community that this adoration creates among like-minded devotees. Fandom, like religion, is social glue. However, the differences between religion and fandom are also important. To say "I worship God" is to make a statement of faith, reverence, and sincerity. To say, "I worship Dolly Parton" is to make a statement that reveals you to be a couple of autographs away from a restraining order. I consider myself to be a rather ordinary fan, not a mad stalker, but perhaps it is all a matter of degree. (I'll return to hyper-fans of Dolly Parton in the next chapter.)

There is an anxiety that attaches to confessing the objects of our admiration. It is exposing. It leaves you open to criticism. Unlike your choice of religion, which is usually respected whatever people's private views, your admiration for a celebrity can invite mockery. "I would rather vomit than listen to Dolly Parton," said my good friend Carrie when I told her about my pilgrimage. I was shocked. Why would she say such a thing? I don't think that it is just the choice of idol that is the issue. It is not simply that Carrie prefers Florence Welch to Dolly Parton. What makes some people awkward is the expression of adoration in and of itself. Being too avid, too intense, is to show oneself to be intemperate, and that makes people feel uncomfortable. We do not have a term that quite articulates this intemperance, this emotional effulgence, but the ancient Greeks did. They called it *akolasia*. *Akolasia* was considered a vice. It was shameful to be excessive and not to be self-possessed. However, being a fan of Dolly Parton has enriched my life. I don't see why I should be ashamed to admit that. That said, I have learned to be careful with whom I share my enthusiasms, at least face-to-face.

Athena and I went from the home of the goddess to homes of the stars (while Tony was keen to stay and experience the Parthenon). I did not feel moved to trace every aspect of Dolly Parton's life, to see, for example, the spot where the Wishy Washy Laundromat once stood, where the eighteen-year-old Dolly was doing her laundry on her first day in Nashville, the day after her classmates at her high school graduation laughed at her ambition to be a star, and there met Carl Dean, her future husband. However, I was curious about where she (and he) now lived and found it hard to resist a bus tour of Homes of the Stars. Gray Line Nashville Sightseeing promised "a driving tour through the neighborhoods of the elite Country Music stars who call Nashville their home" and listed Dolly Parton's house as one of the attractions. And so it was that we found ourselves on a crowded bus in the suffocating heat (the thermometer on the dashboard read 105 degrees) with a vociferously chauvinist bus driver. "Tipper Gore's been on a diet recently," he said of the wife who had just announced her separation from the former vice president and long-time Nashville resident, "She lost a ton of ugly fat. Called Al Gore." As we passed a strip club, "This is where my ex-wife and her three sisters work." Everyone around us laughed nervously and I had a fleeting fantasy of taking over the wheel, Sandra Bullock–style, before the driver made us all sing "Row, Row, Row Your Boat." Things improved slightly when we reached some "homes of the stars." In the swanky suburb of Brentwood in south Nashville we cruised along Curtiswood Lane, aka Millionaire's Row. Our attention was drawn to the governor's mansion, next door to Minnie Pearl's old house (entirely obscured from view by a row of strategically planted trees) and opposite the home, we were told, of Vernon Rudolph, cofounder of Krispy Kreme donuts. Every time the driver pointed out a residence, whether or not the bus had stopped or slowed down, the tourists surged in that direction, cameras flashing. Why would anyone want a photo of the house owned by the cofounder of Krispy Kreme donuts? Or a photo of the many "stars" of whom most of us had clearly never heard? One woman berated her husband loudly when he was not fast enough to snap Martina McBride's house. If he had managed it, all he would have got is a blurred image of columns and a flagpole.

I was saving my lurching and snapping for Dolly Parton's house, which, according to the tour, lies on the Crockett Road. To give you some idea of what this means in the Nashville real estate hierarchy, we were told that the average cost of a house in Nashville is $150,000; the average cost of a house in Brentwood is $450,000; and the average cost of a house in the Crockett Road neighborhood is $800,000. The revelation of each amount prompted an increasingly astonished "ooh!" from the other passengers, while I was reflecting miserably that $800,000 would be lucky to buy you a prefab shack in Santa Barbara. I calculated that it would be less expensive to buy a house in an affluent suburb of Nashville and commute by airplane to Santa Barbara than it would be to buy and live in this small California city. I was so preoccupied with the ridiculousness of this that I almost missed Dolly Parton's house. Dolly calls her house Tara after Scarlett O'Hara's mansion in *Gone with the Wind*, an icon of southern splendor (and an echo of Loretta Lynn's name for her house). The photo I took was worth flattening Athena against the window for, but the house itself is less revealing than the two buildings alongside it, out of range of my camera. If we are to trust our guide (and that is a big *if*), the first of these is a chapel where Dolly renewed her wedding vows. The second is a house for one of her relatives whose job it is to look after her wigs. Having a wig-keeper's house on your property is reassuringly eccentric and diva-like, but this information was accompanied, rather predictably, by an anecdote about Dolly Parton's early poverty. When she was a young girl, the story goes, a hungry Dolly was taken pity upon by a cookie salesman who would give her his wares for free. Many years later, superstar Dolly remembered her kind benefactor and gave him a job selling cookies at her theme park. Once again the present-day wealth of the performer is validated by her earlier poverty, which, once escaped, becomes proof of her noble heart. "The thing about Dolly Parton," affirmed our driver, "she remembers who she is."

The rest of the tour was anticlimactic for me, though not for our fellow passengers, who responded vocally to the snippets of information about their favorite stars. "Keith Urban and Nicole Kidman live in a gated enclosure" (Boo!); "LeAnn Rimes has installed a special elevator in her house for transporting her Christmas decorations" (murmurs of approval); "Brad Paisley once came on board this very tour bus without his shirt on" (wild applause). It was strange to have these tidbits interspersed with more sobering glimpses into the region's history. We passed the Midway Plantation Slave Cemetery, marked with the following sign: "The City of Brentwood restored this cemetery to honor the unsung heroes who came from Africa and labored on the Midway plantation in the 1850's. They survived the horrors of the Middle Passage, endured the shackles of slavery, raised their children, honored their parents and worked hard to make America a better place." The City of Brentwood has some chutzpah. No inconvenient recognition of the routine separation of slaves from their families, and no mention of slave owners. They have recast slavery as a challenging and patriotic career path.

After the tour, the need for water and air conditioning urged us on to our next destination: the Country Music Hall of Fame and Museum (fig. 12). The Country Music Hall of Fame and Museum announces its purpose and good humor through a cluster of architectural symbols, some obvious to all, others

12. The Country Music Hall of Fame and Museum

only to the initiated. The left of the building as you face it is a
5,300-square-foot rotunda with four disc tiers on its roof that
represent the development of recording technology: the 78
rpm disc, the vinyl LP, the 45 rpm disc, and the compact disc.
A pointed metal tower on top evokes WSM radio, the signal
that transmits the Grand Ole Opry shows. Vertical stone bars
around the top of the rotunda's outside wall mark the musical
arrangement to the chorus of the country classic "Will the
Circle Be Unbroken." The main façade of the museum is white,
with long black windows alternately in pairs and threes, as
if a giant invisible hand is unpeeling the rotunda and on the
inside of the peel is revealed a piano keyboard. The peel sweeps
upward on the right of the building to resemble the fin of a
Cadillac, perhaps the solid gold Cadillac that belonged to Elvis
and is now one of the exhibits inside the building, or maybe
the '52 Cadillac in which Hank Williams died mysteriously on
January 1, 1953. Inscribed into the pale stone of the exterior

wall under the sign "Hall of Fame" is a quotation from Merle Haggard: "Country songs are the dreams of the working man." Opened in 2001, the museum still has a sharp new feel to it, and it parades its hipness from all angles. From the air, apparently, it looks like a treble clef.

Inside the rotunda, the refrain WILL THE CIRCLE BE UNBROKEN is spelled out in large gold letters above the commemorative plaques of the members of the Hall of Fame, including Dolly Parton, who was inducted in 1999. It is an odd song to quote, a plangent tale of a child losing her mother but imagining that the family will be one day reunited in heaven. The space inside the rotunda is chapel-like, inspiring people to speak in hushed tones not used elsewhere in the museum, and creating an atmosphere of reverence for the music, its history, and its practitioners. This is in contrast with the main body of the museum, which offers a bright and bracing journey through the history of country music, from the Carter Family to Taylor Swift. I learned much about the two television shows that were instrumental in bringing country artists to national attention, *Hee Haw*, and *The Porter Wagoner Show*. *Hee Haw*, a variety show that ran for over twenty years from 1969, is a throwback to the radio barn dances of the 1940s, whose stereotypes of rural people seem very dated now. The original set of *Hee Haw* is displayed in the museum, with mannequins of grinning country bumpkins in bib overalls standing in a field in fictional Kornfield Kounty. The series is still available on DVD, so you can see how Dolly Parton, luminous in lavender chiffon, gives a lilting performance of "Love Is Like a Butterfly" followed by a heartfelt rendition of her "I Will Always Love You" and transcends what the DVD blurb calls the "pickin' and grinnin', singin' and spinnin' tall tales and corny jokes," as if she comes from another realm entirely.

The Porter Wagoner Show showcased Dolly Parton as Porter Wagoner's duet partner from 1967 to 1974 (the show itself was syndicated from 1960 to 1981). On display are photographs of Porter with his blonde pompadour wearing his famous "Nudie" suits, flamboyant rhinestone-studded outfits in jewel-bright colors designed by tailor Nudie Cohn. Wagoner is singing alongside Dolly Parton, who sported increasingly ostentatious hairstyles and costumes. They were both, to paraphrase a journalist, "peacocks among penguins." RCA records signed Dolly as Porter's duet partner and as a solo artist, and in 1973, as music history would have it, Dolly Parton struck out on her own to become an international superstar.

Given that almost a whole floor of the museum is given over to Hank Williams Sr. and Jr., it was disappointing to find that Dolly Parton does not even get a cabinet to herself. She shares one with Kris Kristofferson and Tom T. Hall, under the heading "When Two Worlds Collide: Country Meets Mass Market." Kris Kristofferson is renowned as a singer, actor, and songwriter (he cowrote "Me and Bobby McGee"), but I had never heard of Tom T. Hall. It turns out that he wrote "Harper Valley PTA," the fabulous exposé of small-town hypocrisy and meanness sung by Jeannie C. Riley and later by Dolly Parton, but neither he nor Kristofferson are as big a star as Dolly.

It is an interesting decision to display her contribution in this way. "Mass market," with its connotations of corporate and undiscriminating business, is an ambivalent way of saying "mainstream" or "popular." Country music has policed its boundaries fiercely. The stunt pulled by country singer Charlie Rich at the 1975 Country Music Awards is a notorious example of hostility to the mainstream. Before he announced that John Denver had won Entertainer of the Year award he set fire to the envelope on stage. This was widely interpreted as a protest against Denver being too "pop" and not enough "country." As hits like "Here You Come Again" brought her to a new, wider audience, Dolly Parton had to defend herself against critics with the repeated reassurance, "I haven't left country—I'm taking it with me." She also provoked controversy when she went to Hollywood to take on the role of Doralee in the movie *9 to 5*, for which she wrote the theme song. At the time, it was a bold and brave move beyond her expected generic niche. Now, however, "Country Meets Mass Market" seems oddly anachronistic. It makes little sense at a time when Taylor Swift has become a musical phenomenon, the top-selling digital artist in history, and Billboard and Nielsen SoundScan's top-selling artist twice in three years (2008 and 2010). Taylor Swift is both country and mass-market, but without Dolly Parton there would have been no Taylor Swift. Why not have an exhibit celebrating how Dolly broke new ground and paved the way for later artists?

There is a video installation in the museum called "Taking Back and Singing It Out" that acknowledges the role that country music songs and musicians have played in politics. It focuses on key songs: "The Ballad of Ira Hayes," the Johnny Cash song about a Pima Indian who fought for his country; "Stand by Your Man" by Tammy Wynette, which occasioned feminist ire and an embarrassing moment for Hillary Clinton in 1992 when she said after the Gennifer Flowers debacle that she "wasn't some little Tammy Wynette, standing by her man," prompting the singer to retort, "I think that's what you're doing, don't you?"; "Okie from Muskogee," Merle Haggard's political satire; "The Pill," by Loretta Lynn; "Independence Day," Martina McBride's song about domestic violence; and "Courtesy of the Red, White, and Blue," rousing nationalism from Toby Keith ("you'll be sorry that you messed with the U. S. of A., 'cause we'll put a boot in your ass—it's the American way"). Songs like "Courtesy of the Red, White, and Blue" have led to the reputation of country music as a uniquely Republican genre, but why should patriotism, even crudely expressed patriotism, be the sole province of Republicans? Songs like "The Ballad of Ira Hayes" show that the politics of country music are more diverse and thoughtful than they are sometimes represented to be.

However, there are some striking absences from the

Country Music Hall of Fame and Museum, and one wonders whether politics has played a role here. Where is k. d. lang, the Canadian singer who performed with her Patsy Cline tribute band, the Reclines, and went on to commercial success and to win a number of awards, including a Grammy for Best Female Performance for her 1989 album *Absolute Torch and Twang?* The first country singer to come out as a lesbian, lang has so effectively been written out of the picture that Chely Wright can claim to be first openly gay female singer all over again. It was k. d. lang's aggressive vegetarianism that is said to have most upset the Nashville bigwigs. Her "Meat Stinks" campaign hardly fits with the "huntin' and fishin'" image of the country lifestyle. The Dixie Chicks are another obvious absence, and it is hard not to suspect that they are being ostracized from the museum because of lead singer Natalie Maines's criticism of George W. Bush for America's invasion of Iraq in 2003, which provoked a storm of controversy. It seemed to us that the Country Music Hall of Fame and Museum does more than celebrate country music and preserve its history. In policing who is in and who is out, it strong-arms artists in the industry to toe the country line.

Toward the end of our tour, I spotted a poster inconspicuously placed behind a television screen (fig. 13). It showed Dolly Parton dressed as the Statue of Liberty, with the words "Spirit of '76" underneath her image. It is the poster that accompanied an issue of *Country Music Magazine*. Pasted onto the poster was a proclamation by former president Gerald R. Ford, and I had to squeeze myself behind the television set to read it:

A PROCLAMATION
Country music is a descriptive and entertaining chronicle of American life. The melodies and lyrics of a country song are drawn from the very heart of America and its people. The music reflects the joys and sorrows of daily life and it reminds us that truth, compassion and moral character should guide

13. The poster of Dolly with president Gerald R. Ford's
proclamation on the left-hand side

our actions and shape our beliefs. Country music is the spirit
of America in song. It has grown in popularity among a wide
range of people in all walks of life.

It is a uniquely American life form. Which will flourish as
long as the story of our nation is the story of common people.
It is fitting that we pay tribute to the music, to the hundreds of
talented people who perform it, and to the millions more who
enjoy it. Now, therefore, I, GERALD R. FORD, President of the
United States of America, designate October 1976 as Country
Music Month and encourage all Americans to commemo-
rate this designation with suitable observances. IN WITNESS
WHEREOF, I have here unto set my hand this 29th day of September in the year of our lord nineteen hundred and seventy
six and of the independence of the United States of America
the two hundred and first.

Gerald R. Ford

This extraordinary proclamation, at least from a foreign perspective (I cannot imagine a British prime minister declaring September "Britpop month"), echoed the sentiments of Richard Nixon when he appeared on the Grand Ole Opry show in 1974 and lauded country music for representing "the heart of America." "Country music makes America a better country," he declared. Some years later, George H. Bush explained his love of the genre by comparing it to "a Norman Rockwell painting": "It captures the essence of the American spirit and portrays experiences that those who work hard and play by the rules can identify with. . . . To me, the same qualities that make country music so appealing have also made our country great."

I had not previously given much thought to country music as essentially and uniquely American. After all, my father, who called it "our music," was Greek Cypriot. Nor had I made the crucial connection that follows this insight: in making a pilgrimage to a country music star I was necessarily making a pilgrimage into the heart of America itself, literally and imaginatively. (Less an Aha! moment than a Duh! moment for those more knowledgeable about country music, no doubt, but it was a startling realization for me.) This was to be more than a pilgrimage to Dollywood. The pilgrimage and the music that had prompted it was a metonym for a more profound journey of discovery, one about identity and belonging, and our country, our new home.

In the café in the museum lobby, Tony and I discussed whether country music has a unique claim to being essentially American. I suggested that you could insert *rap* into Gerald Ford's proclamation, if not in 1974, then today. There seems an obvious case for saying that rap is essentially American, even if its popularity goes beyond that. And does not rap also tell the story of "common people"? Tony countered that country music alone is associated with the cult of individualism in the West. With the *cowboy*. "This is uniquely American," he insisted. "After all, English culture doesn't have cowboys. In English culture, cowboys are always gay. The singing cowboy of the films I used to watch in the fifties is American: country music is American."

Our conversation that afternoon in the calm interior of the museum came back to me a few weeks later. I was browsing YouTube and came across the video to a duet Dolly Parton performed with the British pop band Culture Club called "Your Kisses Are Charity." Boy George, the lead singer of Culture Club, was a hero of my youth. My father was so shocked at his wearing makeup and flamboyant robes that my sisters and I were ordered to switch off the television whenever he came on. "Your Kisses Are Charity" is a catchy song in which Dolly's high, lilting tones beautifully frame Boy George's lower, mellower ones. Dolly performed on the music show *Top of the Pops* with Culture Club (towered over by Boy George), but does not appear in the official video of the song. I wonder if there is a story behind her absence. In Dolly Parton's stead, acting as a visual stand-in representing country, are semiclad, line-dancing cowboys and cowgirls. The cowgirls are wearing blue bikini tops, fringed skirts, and cowboy hats and boots. But it is the cowboys who are the stars of this video. With naked torsos and kerchiefs round their necks, they touch the rims of their cowboy hats and slap their butts playfully, like a Kenny Chesney stripper troupe flanking Boy George as he pouts in lipstick and glittering eye shadow. When interviewed on CMT news in 1999 about the incongruous partnership, Dolly Parton stressed the musical appeal of the song: "The song is so good and they even used a lot of country instruments on it like mandolin and fiddle" and deflected potential criticism with her trademark humor: "He outdid me on the makeup! . . . I kind of got jealous because he had outdressed me." But her bottom line, "I'm in the Hall of Fame now and they can't kick me out!" is telling (fig. 14).

At the heart of "Music City, USA" and by far the most important institution in country music is the *Grand Ole Opry*.

14. Dolly's star outside the County Music Hall of Fame and Museum

It is America's longest-running radio show, and is now also
frequently televised. Dolly Parton first visited the *Opry* when
she was eleven years old, and she made a guest appearance
two years later. Ten years after that, the *Opry* invited her to
be a permanent cast member. Since 1974 the *Opry* has been
broadcast from the Grand Ole Opry House east of downtown
Nashville. I had hoped that the flood damage sustained in May
would have been repaired by June, foolishly, as it turned out:
the *Opry* was not to open again until late September. Most of
its shows were moved to the Ryman Auditorium, one of the
Opry's former homes. However, I very much wanted to see the
Grand Ole Opry House, maybe to get a glimpse of the hallowed
stage, even if it was being repaired. We did not even get close.
We found the complex, ignored the large "closed" signs, and
drove up to the guard's hut at the entrance. I wound down the
window. "I know that you're closed, but I'm a huge fan of the

Opry and I've come all the way from England just to see it," I
lied in my best porcelain English accent.

"I'm sorry, Madam, but we are closed and no one is allowed
in," came the reply.

"Is there any way you might be persuaded to let me just
take a quick peek?" I pleaded, taking some notes out of my wal-
let. (This once worked a treat in an Italian museum).

"We are closed and no one is allowed in," said the guard
more firmly.

"But I am a huge Dolly Parton fan and I really *need* to see the
Opry" was my last, pathetic attempt before Tony revved the car
into reverse and we headed back to downtown Nashville.

★   ★   ★

The sky-blue façade and looped pink neon tube lighting that
spells out Dolly's distinctive signature and butterfly trademark
gives Dolly Parton's Trinkets and Treasures store a distinctive
façade in the historic 2nd Avenue District of downtown Nashville. Inside is a visual feast: candy colors on the walls, sparkly
costumes in display cases, and the twinkling of necklaces,
bracelets, photo frames, and other goodies. Athena and I were
entranced. "I'm rather thirsty," announced Tony and he went
off to check out the Wildhorse Saloon next door. Trinkets and
Treasures is like Claire's Accessories for adults. It is cheap and
cheerful and promotes Dolly as a brand more than as a singer.
There were no CDs on display when we went, though you could
buy DVDs of concert performances. Instead, there were Dolly
mugs, a red one with "I will always love you," and a blue one
with "Pour myself a cup of ambition." There were bandanas and
buttons, tote bags and posters, with rhinestones and butterflies
and, of course, images of Dolly on them. Among these were T-
shirts, some of which depicted Dolly, and some with slogans on
them: *Dumb Blonde* (actually DumԘ BlOnDɘ), *Hick*, and *White
Trash* (figs. 15 and 16). Who would wear a T-Shirt with *White
Trash* on it, and what would they think they were saying?

15, 16. T-Shirts on sale at Trinkets and Treasures

Famously, and, as it turned out, incorrectly, the filmmaker John Waters said in August 1994, "In six months, no one will say 'white trash.' . . . It's the last racist thing you can say and get away with." You can still get away with it; *white trash* is used as a term of abuse, like "hillbilly" or "hick" but with stronger insinuations about lack of moral character. Take this comment, written in response to a report in *US Weekly* online on the opening of the Trinkets and Treasures store: "Great now her trashy treasures will be for sell, Dolly is nothing but hillbilly trash and anyone who takes a junky journey through are store is trash too, but white trash tend to like . . . well white trash!" ("Carrie Underwood," March 12, 2010, 2:21 p.m.). The sloppy spelling and the joke pseudonym do not mask the straightforward hostility of these words. It is a hostility given heft by a long and unpleasant history of the phrase and its usage. The earliest recorded usage of *white trash* is in the early nineteenth century in the context of black slavery and white servitude, but tracing its origins to the insults of black slaves toward white servants, as historians often do, may be too convenient. It is, at any rate, an explanation that exonerates whites of higher social status who have benefited from the social hierarchy.

As so often with racial and class prejudice, the view that rural poor whites were different from their richer and urban counterparts was given strength and legitimacy by science, or rather pseudo-science, in the form of "Eugenic Family Studies," research produced from 1880 to 1920 which sought to prove scientifically that poor whites living in the country were "genetic defectives." Genealogies were traced back to "defective" sources, usually a person of mixed blood. (The pride of Loretta Lynn and Elvis Presley in their mixed-race ancestry would have damned them as "defective" and the epitome of "white trash" according to these studies). Family clans like "The Jukes" and "The Kallikaks" piqued public prurience, and the image of these people as stupid, filthy, and sexual-deviant criminals made a strong and political impact. As sociologists

Matt Wray and Annalee Newitz explain in their study *White Trash: Race and Class in America,*

> The eugenic family studies had a very pronounced influence on social policy and medical practice in the early 20th century. Conservative politicians used them effectively as propaganda in their call to end all forms of welfare and private giving to the poor. The burgeoning medical and psychiatric establishments used them to enlarge their fields, resulting in the involuntary sterilization and forced institutionalization of large numbers of poor rural whites. While the adoption of eugenic theory and practice by the Nazis in 1930s and 1940s did much to discredit eugenics in the United States, the stereotypes of rural poor whites as incestuous and sexually promiscuous, violent, alcoholic, lazy, and stupid remain with us to this day.

Wearing a T-Shirt that says "White Trash" involves more than a pinch of historical amnesia.

In contrast, the British term *chav*, used to denigrate working-class youth (typically, but not exclusively, used of white people), is a recently coined insult. Its first recorded usages stem from the beginning of the twenty-first century, although the term is said to originate in a nineteenth-century Romany word *chavi*, meaning "child." Other explanations are that it is an acronym for Council House Average Vermin ("council house" being the rough equivalent of accommodation provided by welfare), or that it stands for "Chatham average," a reference to Chatham, a town in Kent widely perceived to have a hub of antisocial youth. Unlike the white-trash stereotype, which targets the moral failings of poor whites, the chav stereotype is aimed at working-class aspiration. It derides low-income youth who wear branded sportswear, designer labels, and gold jewelry, an attitude that is as much about keeping people in their place as it is about taste. *Chav* and *white trash* are both slurs against impoverished social groups, but they have quite different characterizations and histories.

The White Trash T-shirt presumes some knowingness on the part of its wearer. Cultural critic Gael Sweeney misguidedly distinguishes *white trash* from *camp* on the grounds that *camp* is knowing and *white trash* is not:

> Unlike Camp, which is an aesthetic of the urban, elite, and gay sensibility, White Trash has its roots in the south, the denigrated product of a rural-based under-class of poor whites. . . . The gay sensibility may read itself into White Trash, but White Trash doesn't comprehend the gay sensibility, the realm of Camp. Camp is elitist, of the upper middle class and urban, while White Trash is rooted in the rural and working class. White Trash is sincere, where Camp is deliberate and parodic. . . . Camp and White Trash may buy the same portrait of Elvis and hang it proudly in the living room, but Camp displays it as parody, to outrage the dominant taste, while White Trash displays it because it is so beautiful.

For Sweeney, the paradigm of white trash is Dolly Parton, whom she contrasts with the late drag queen Divine: "Divine was an icon of Camp; Dolly Parton is an icon of White Trash; both privilege big hair, gold lamé, and exaggerated bodies, but Divine was a drag parody of a 'trashy' woman, while Dolly's persona grew out of a Kentucky backwoods child's naïve idea of glamour."

There are several problems with this analysis. To present, as an idée fixe, that an object or person is to be viewed one way, as intelligent, witty, and knowing, because the person who views it is urban, elite, and engaged with gay culture, whereas it will be viewed in the opposite way, as ignorant, sincere, and naïve, because the viewer is rural, working class, and not engaged with gay culture, is to reinstate prejudice rather than explain it. It also allows gay men to have all the fun.

Sweeney's model also fails to take into account social mobility. Am I white trash? When I asked this question of my friend David, he laughed and said "Helen, you've been reading the *National Enquirer* for the last fifteen years." So I have, but I've also been reading the *Times Literary Supplement*. I have a poster of Dolly in my office and am always delighted when that surprises people, but I also think it is beautiful. Can you be white trash with a PhD? I decided to test myself against one of the many online checklists that define the category:

A white person (particularly American) who demonstrates some of the following traits:

1. Listens to Country and Western (Yes)
2. Lives in a trailer or poorly kept apartment. (So-so: I live in an apartment that is poorly kept by the landlady, but well kept by us)
3. Very stupid/uneducated (I am sure I am often stupid, but I am not uneducated)
4. On welfare or uses food stamps (No)
5. Is overweight (Yes, considerably)
6. Has bad health (Not sure; not awful health, but not good either)
7. Has bigoted or racist opinion of other people (No, I hope not)
8. Has sex often (What counts as often? Yes, OK, as often as possible)
9. Watches violent films on television (You bet)
10. Likes Vodka and Mountain Dew (Yes! What's not to like?)

I score at least 5 out of 10 on this white-trash test. Is that a pass or not?

Sweeney's biggest mistake, however, is to read Dolly Parton as naïve, rather than knowing, about her self-presentation. The White Trash T-shirt demonstrates her knowingness. The

joke is that while in some ways Dolly may be "trashy," in other
ways the label is clearly inappropriate, given that she is now an
international superstar who has written over four thousand
songs and is reputed to be worth a quarter of a billion dollars.
This is the contradiction that is recognized in one of her say-
ings, "It costs a lot to look this cheap," and in the Dumb Blonde
T-Shirt worn by Dolly at the store's grand opening that quotes
from her song of the same title: "Just because I'm blonde, don't
think I'm dumb, 'cause this dumb blonde is nobody's fool."
The biography of Dolly Parton by Stephen Miller plays on this
contradiction: it is called *Smart Blonde*. It is a repeated motif
of Dolly's to acknowledge that under the glitz lies a heart and
mind, and that it is a mistake to judge her by a stereotype:

> *I'm just a Backwoods Barbie, too much make-up, too much hair;*
> *Don't be fooled by thinkin' that the goods are not all there.*
> . . .
> *I've always been misunderstood because of how I look;*
> *Don't judge me by the cover 'cause I'm a real good book.*

When Dolly tells the anecdote about how she entered a Dolly
Parton lookalike contest, but lost to a drag queen, and when
she quips "If I hadn't been a woman I'd have been a drag
queen," she shows not just a sense of humor but knowing self-
parody.

There is something audacious about Dolly Parton's refusal
to break away from what she has called her "country girl's
idea of glamor." In the same vein, there may be something
daring about wearing a White Trash T-shirt. It is a refusal to
deny class differences, and an attempt to reclaim the term as
a gesture of defiance (much as other insults—queer, bitch,
etc.—have been blunted by embracing them, with varying
degrees of success). In his autobiography, rap singer Eminem
reflects on the early days of his career when he was angry all
the time: "Part of it was that people had started referring to me

as trailer-park trash. I went with that perception, because I felt like I did represent that . . . I mean, I was basically poor white trash. If that's what I'm going to be labeled as, then I might as well represent it to the fullest. I thought, Fuck it, I'm just going to go all out with it." Eminem's is a fierce articulation of what Dolly Parton and other country artists express with a dash of humor. Gretchen Wilson explains that she called her autobiography *Redneck Woman* so as to show who a real "redneck woman" is, to move beyond the stereotypes. She writes: "In many parts of the country, 'redneck' is an acceptable slur, along with equally acceptable put-downs like 'white trash' and 'hillbilly.' Low-income rural whites are about the last people in America who seem to be fair game for blatant stereotyping. Even media personalities who know better regularly refer to Britney Spears as a white-trash queen or to a NASCAR fan as a (dumb) redneck." Her punch line reclaims the insult: "Like I, or any self-respecting redneck, could give a good rat's ass." Toby Keith also turned the slur in on itself when he called his 2006 album *White Trash with Money*, an echo of the song of the same title by country rock band Confederate Railroad. Here is the song's refrain:

> Well, I mighta been born just poor white trash,
> But I sold a million records, made a little cash.
> The doctors and the lawyers don't think it's funny
> That they're living next door to white trash with money.
> . . .
> Say, honey, what do you think about a couple of pink flamingoes
> Out in the front yard?

This is clearly parodic. It is a strategy occasionally employed elsewhere. When Sarah Palin wore a T-Shirt that said "Proud to be Valley Trash," she was doing more than publicizing a Wasilla website that advertises "trash" (cars, computers, "guns and ammo"); she was playing on, and cocking a sneer at, the insults leveled at her for being "white trash," such as Erica Jong's snooty *Huffington Post* article, "White Trash America certainly has allure for voters."

Moreover, in her autobiography, Dolly discusses her desire, as a girl, to look like a model in a magazine, and she presents a more complicated, and rather different idea of "trashiness" than has previously been recognized:

> Womanhood was a difficult thing to get a grip on in those hills, unless you were a man. My sisters and I used to cling desperately to anything halfway feminine. . . . We could see the pictures of the models in the newspapers that lined the walls of our house and the occasional glimpse we would get at a magazine. We wanted to look like them. They didn't look at all like they had to work in the fields. They didn't look like they had to take a spit bath in a dishpan. They didn't look as if men and boys could just put their hands on them any time they felt like it, and with any degree of roughness they chose. The way they looked, if a man wanted to touch them, he'd better be damned nice to them.

In her account, looking like a model was a means of ensuring better behavior from men. The women who looked ordinary and plain were subjected to harassment and sexual assault; they were treated, in other words, as if they were trash. Looking like a model or the town hooker (as Dolly tells the story in other anecdotes) was a strategy to escape being treated like trash. In this narrative, dressing in a feminine way was an empowering act, a way out of a life of disrespect and misery. Who wouldn't want to put that on a T-shirt?

I did not buy the White Trash T-shirt. The designer and wearer might be knowingly arch about its slogan, but who's to say that people looking at it will be? I bought one with the names of a hundred of Dolly's hits on it instead.

5

Tennessee Mountain Homes

A flyer for the Country Music Hall of Fame and Museum has a motto in bold white letters underneath its distinctive "record" logo:

all ROADS *lead*

H O M E

Just follow the music

We were hoping that all roads today would lead to Dolly Parton's childhood homes, places that I wanted to visit before the climax of Dollywood. It was a sweltering June morning already rumbling with the promise of an evening storm, and the road we were taking was I-40 East. When she was growing up, Dolly Parton's family lived in a number of places in and around what is now the Great Smoky Mountains National Park. So we were heading for the easternmost part of the state, to the jagged edge that separates Tennessee from North Carolina, like two sides of a torn-off ticket.

Dolly Parton's music is preoccupied with home, with leaving home, returning home, and longing for home. Her album *My Tennessee Mountain Home*, originally released in 1973, is a paean to her childhood home and to rural Tennessee. To listen to it from start to finish as we did on the two-hour drive from Nashville to Pigeon Forge, is to acquire an imaginative version, a poetic map if you like, of the physical reality that we were going to see. It is also to get a glimpse of Dolly Parton's attachment to her childhood home, and what it cost her to leave it in pursuit of a better life. It is specific in its autobiographical recollections, with the letter that she wrote to her parents on first moving to Nashville, and with a song that pays tribute to the doctor who delivered her ("Dr. Robert F. Thomas"), but universal in its intense nostalgia for the lost past, "being mugged by melancholy," as Tony put it.

Dolly's songs repeatedly conjure images of home that are characterized by nature. Her lyrics describe the settings for her mountain cabins and cottages with picturesque and pastoral imagery: the banks of the Little Pigeon River, fields of green, swimming holes, clear blue streams, meadows "where the meadow lark is sitting in the tree," possum grapes, muskadines, "the aster and the dahlia and wild geraniums' drops of morning dew still linger[ing] on the iris leaves," honeysuckle, and "the sacred blossoms of the dogwood tree." Birds and insects flit and swoop and provide a pastoral soundscape: "crickets singing," June bugs and "glowin' fireflies," "bob-whites callin'," black crows cawkin', eagles, sparrows, hummingbirds, dirt dobbers and whippoorwills. Dolly Parton's is an Emersonian view of nature, in which home is the essence of nature, and nature is nurturing. Take the first verse of another song on the *My Tennessee Mountain Home* album, "Wrong Direction Home":

> *In a shingle covered cottage at the foothills of the smokies*
> *Near a mountain stream that's flowing crystal clear*
> *Where the humming birds and honey bees feed on Mama's roses*
> *My mem'ries just grow sweeter with the years.*
> *Mem'ries of my childhood are as sweet as mountain honey*
> *And as fresh as dew on morning glory vines;*
> *I grew up surrounded by the sights and sounds of nature*
> *And they're forever present in my mind.*

Nature *is* Dolly's home here, as much if not more than the "family that I'm longing to see," who are mentioned in the final verse.

The equation of home and nature in Dolly Parton's songs is reflected in the more widespread characterization of country music as essentially natural. In the words of George D. Hay, the first announcer at the Grand Ole Opry, country music is as "fundamental as sunshine and rain, snow and wind, and the light of the moon peeping through the trees." Johnny Cash was more laconic when he called it "close to nature." A key part of the characterization of country music as "natural" is the idea that country music is distinctively simple, fundamental, and unpremeditated, part of its image as the genre that "keeps it real." Moreover, the repeated associations between country music, home, and nature forge imaginative links between the three. As the Country Music Hall of Fame and Museum flyer implies, it is the music itself that offers the most acute experience of this ideal of home. No physical reality can ever live up to it, hence the inevitable turn to the melancholic. Dolly's songs about home stir up feelings of homesickness, what critic Cecelia Tichi has described as "an unquenchable thirst, a chronic hunger . . . feelings of yearning and desire [that] become a kind of sweet pain." Perhaps this is why my father, a Greek immigrant in England, and years later I myself, an English immigrant to North America, should claim this as "our music"; it is the music of the deracinated, of those searching for a home.

"It's not going to be like *Little House on the Prairie*, is it?" said a small voice from the back of the car. I had made a big mistake in reading Athena the *Little House on the Prairie* in preparation for the trip, remembering the classic children's novel as a warming tale of hearth and heart and completely forgetting the scene in the opening pages where Pa skins and cures animal carcasses. Athena reacted as if I had chosen *The Silence of the Lambs* as her bedtime story. It was not the introduction to American rural life that I had planned. We drove past Knoxville and I relayed to Tony Knoxville trivia that I had picked up. It was once known as the "Underwear Capital of America," and Cormac McCarthy and Quentin Tarantino were both born there. If you listen carefully to the "father's watch" sequence in *Pulp Fiction*, you will catch references to Knoxville. In *Buffy the Vampire Slayer* the evil preacher Caleb, agent of the First, worked in Knoxville before he moved to Sunnydale (a fictionalized Santa Barbara). I wasn't sure what any of this added up to, but I was curious to visit the city. It was not to be: Tony drove on for another half hour, until we were less than an hour away, he estimated, from Pigeon Forge. We stopped for sodas and a bathroom break at a fried chicken joint just off the highway.

Opposite the restaurant was a nondescript building with a sign identifying it as the Calvary Baptist Church and School, and another sign beneath it in admonitory capitals: WHORE-MONGERS AND ADULTERERS GOD WILL JUDGE. HE-BREWS 13.4 (fig. 17). "What's a whoremonger, Mum?" asked Athena. Actually, she mispronounced it "What's a warmonger?" which is a lot easier a question to answer a nine-year-old. "Well, it means that men who, erm, have sex with women who are not their wives, well, God will judge them." "Like Simon Cowell?" "I don't think Simon Cowell is married." "No, judges them like Simon Cowell?" "Not really." (Though I can see a glaring gap in reality TV here). "More like decides how bad they've been and punishes them accordingly." "You and Dad aren't married. Is Dad a whoremonger?" (Parents in unison) "Right—back in the car."

I knew that Tennessee was part of what is called the Bible Belt, but the sheer number of churches lining the highways was still a surprise. We started to count them but quickly gave up; along one stretch of road there was alternately a church, then a fast food place, church, fast food, church, fast food. But even this gradually changing landscape cannot prepare you for

17. Admonition from one of Tennessee's many churches

the outlandish weirdness of Pigeon Forge. It comes upon you
as if you've taken a wrong turn into a drive-in fairground. The
main road, the Parkway, the same road along which the annual
Dolly procession marches, is lined with oversized attractions:
Jurassic Jungle Boat Ride, Reagan's House of Pancakes, Rock
and Fossil Museum, Hillbilly Village, Smoky Mountain Car
Museum, Speed Zone Fun Park, Huck Finn's Catfish Restaurant. Among them is a church advertised by a mammoth cross.
Here even religion has become a fairground attraction. The

exaggerated size of the attractions was disorientating. Robbed of our normal perspective we felt overwhelmed and child-like. Some of the entertainments take delight in breaking the visitor's expectations of realism and scale. The Titanic ("The World's Largest Museum Attraction") is a gargantuan ocean liner that looks at first sight as if it is going to sail full steam into the highway. The Smoky Mountain Fantasy Golf has an enormous fanged sea monster that appears to be poised to strike the passing motorists. This is schlock, to be sure, but on a first encounter it is disturbing schlock. Amusement parks play with their visitors' perspectives. Dollywood in Pigeon Forge is an amusement park set within an amusement park.

We pressed on through to Gatlinburg, slighter smaller than Pigeon Forge (with a population of around 4,000 to Pigeon Forge's 6,000), another tourist town with two major boasts. One is that it is "The Gateway to the Smoky Mountains." Indeed, the town owes its growth to the establishment of the Great Smoky Mountains National Park in 1934. Before that it was an agricultural region, and then, in the early 1900s, it developed a timber industry. The other is that Gatlinburg is the second-most popular "destination wedding" location in the States, after Las Vegas. Ripley's is big here: Ripley's Believe it or Not! Museum, Ripley's Aquarium of the Smokies, Ripley's Super Fun Zone, Ripley's David Crockett Mini Golf. There are also less predictable attractions like Christ in the Smokies Museum and Gardens ("Journey through life-size scenes of the story of Christ featuring dramatic figures, mood lighting, in-spirational music, special effects and memorable narrations"), and the unforgettable Salt and Pepper Shaker Museum ("In wedding-friendly Gatlinburg, it also provides a one-of-a-kind location to say your vows, complete with commemorative salt-and-pepper shakers to take home"). I know that it is easy to deride the commercialism and tackiness of Gatlinburg, but I was secretly thrilled. It screamed *fun* in a way that the worthy-but-dull holiday destinations of my childhood, National Trust cottages in the grounds of English stately homes, with no TV or central heating, rarely did.

There is no place in Dolly's music for the retail pleasures of Pigeon Forge and Gatlinburg. It is true that many of the businesses must have sprung up long after the childhood celebrated in Dolly Parton's songs, long after Dolly, at six, was baptized in the Little Pigeon River, which is now a popular place for rafting. But the absence of these towns in her music, a striking absence when you go there and experience their vibrant palpability, is as ideological as it is realistic. In a nutshell, her songs tell us again and again that the city is as bad as the country is good. Sometimes it is a necessary evil, necessary because of the need to leave home and go to the city in pursuit of a better life. Homesickness and nostalgia for the country life left behind is at the center of "Appalachian Memories," "Heartsong," "Wrong Direction Home," "The Greatest Days of All," "Tennessee Homesick Blues," "Take Me Back," and "Smoky Mountain Memories." "I'm a Drifter" makes it clear that the wandering life is not one of exciting road trips and adventures. Instead, it conflates being nomadic with feeling empty.

Other songs imagine characters rejecting their city lives and going back home. This is the scenario in *When the Sun Goes Down Tomorrow* and *Back Home*, which is both title and refrain:

> Back home, back home, yes, I'm going back home
> To the factory smoke and city life, I'm sayin' "So long."
> I've shed a lot of tears through all these years that I've been gone,
> And I've spent a lot of time a-wishin' I could go back home.

Repeatedly the country is represented as nurturing, in contrast to the shallow materialism of the city, a construction that has a long history in politics and literature. Ancient Roman pastoral and elegy played on the same themes, but in modern times it is probably most associated with the French critic and historian Alexis de Tocqueville. However, even de

Tocqueville did not conjure some of the tragic scenarios found in other Dolly Parton songs that tell of life "out there in this big ol' world," where "reality takes hold" and "dreams can turn to nightmares" ("Chasing Rainbows"). These songs tell of leaving the country in search of wealth, but here the choice to leave home is not presented as a necessary evil, but rather a foolish decision that causes pain and ends in loss or death. In "Kentucky Gambler" a coalminer leaves his wife and children in Kentucky for the casinos of Nevada. He loses his money and, when someone else has taken his place in Kentucky, he loses his family too. "Bluer Pastures" portrays a girl who leaves her Kentucky home with big dreams and the desire for riches and in doing so breaks her lover's heart. When her new life does not work out she returns to the country humbled and anxious, hoping she'll be welcomed back home.

"Blackie Kentucky" puts a much darker spin on this parable. A woman leaves her hometown seduced by a stranger's "promise of riches" and the desire to "know something better than sad poverty." She ends up "in a mansion with a husband who never loved me" and who controls her life, neither allowing her family and friends to visit ("because they are country and poor, he's ashamed"), nor allowing her to leave. "If I could come back home," sings the character to the family she cannot see, "I'd never leave you any more. I'd like to see my poor heart work in a coal mine with Daddy." The song ends rather abruptly, with her telling us that she'll leave a note and that her last request will be to be buried in Blackie Kentucky. This is a song of spousal abuse leading to suicide (the woman's only means, as she sees it, of returning home), but it is also a cautionary tale of what might happen to those who leave the country and move to the city. Of course, in real life, husbands treat their wives badly in the country too.

"The city" in Dolly Parton's songs is represented as being far away from the country, either through vague references to "the North" or precise ones to Nevada, Nashville, New

Orleans, and the Big Apple. However, the physical geography of the real world, in which Gatlinburg and Pigeon Forge abut the national park and outlying rural communities, belies the imaginative geography of the songs and their uncomplicated separations between country and city. Are the people who work in Pigeon Forge and Gatlinburg country people or city people? These distinctions are messier than Dolly Parton (or Alexis de Tocqueville) allows. It is also hard not to feel uncomfortable about the relentless idealization of poverty. Rarely do those leading lives of poverty enthuse about its joys; far more often it is those who have escaped hardship, or who have never experienced that way of living, who romanticize it.

Moreover, nostalgia for the past can blind us to the difficulties of the here and now, or, as a character in Woody Allen's *Midnight in Paris* puts it, "Nostalgia is denial, denial of the painful present." Poverty is still much evident in the communities of Sevier County, but it is easier, perhaps, for us to reminisce about the prettified poverty of times past than to worry about those working for minimum wage in the fast food joints of Pigeon Forge. Collectively, Dolly Parton's songs that are nostalgic for the simple life are reactionary, telling us not to want too much and to be wary of challenging the status quo, a rather different message than that which is promoted in songs like "Change It." Most strikingly, this ideology is in stark contrast to the life lived by Dolly Parton herself. Dolly left home when she was young, and no matter how many weekends she may now spend in the mountains, she chooses to live in cities and as a businesswoman. As she says in the lyrics to "The Sacrifice":

I was gonna be rich no matter how much it cost,
And I was gonna win no matter how much I lost.

Dolly illustrates the paradox that in order to be a success, in her terms (a success built in part on her songs about the country), leaving home and going to the city were necessary and brought her and her family huge gains as well as disadvantages. She is able to miss her past, from the position of a comfortable present and future, and to miss the country from the luxury of her city homes. There is a tension, therefore, between some of her songs and her example.

I had booked us into the Bear Creek Inn with a "renovation special" package, a risky decision, but the construction work was not too disruptive. The hotel was not the Peabody, but it continued the animal theming with bear motifs everywhere, including stuffed bear heads mounted in the lobby, which upset Athena. Anticipating the needs of the newlyweds who make up a sizeable amount of their custom, the hotel, like most in Gatlinburg, had a Jacuzzi tub large enough for two in the spacious bedroom. It was also equipped with a large-screen TV, and effective faux log fire. A small wrought iron balcony offered a view of the Little Pigeon River from the third floor. Athena thought that a Jacuzzi in the main room was the "coolest thing ever," and splashed about in it for hours, while Tony and I ordered pizza from across the road and watched a television report about a controversy over a Knox school board textbook that refers to creationism as "biblical myth." The word "myth" had caused such heated controversy that the school board had agreed to write to the book's publishers and request that the term be removed. We spent the rest of the afternoon and evening huddled in our room, listening to the thunderstorm that had finally broken crack and bend the trees and churn the river below.

By the following morning the rain had stopped, but moisture was still steaming off the trees in the Smoky Mountains National Park, as if the forest itself were evaporating. We ventured into the park, whose entrance was only a few minutes from our hotel by car. We joined the line of vehicles that crept along the main routes and slowed to a halt when someone spotted a black bear or a fawn. When I look back on this now I am embarrassed: it seems ridiculous to experience a natural wonder from the inside of a car, but for whatever reason—fatigue, heat, laziness, or fear of bears (the Park excites visitors with terrifying warnings about encounters with bears)—we spent a good four hours driving around the park. We meandered around the eleven-mile loop to Cades Cove Historic District, a broad, lush valley framed by mountains. In Cades Cove there was evidence that the area had relatively recently been populated: three churches, barns, log cabins, and a gristmill. There were no signs of the earliest inhabitants, the Cherokee Indians, who lived or hunted in these grounds for hundreds of years, but records show that around 1820 immigrants came from Europe and settled in the valley. Today, no one is allowed to live in the park. I was curious about what had happened to the people who used to live there, the people who once worshipped in the churches and lived in the log cabins that now looked like an empty film set.

The Parton family was among those who used to live in what is now national park land; they moved to the hamlets of Greenbrier and then Locust Ridge after the establishment of the park in 1940, six years before Dolly was born. To my knowledge, there is little recorded about the early Parton family's motivations for and reactions to relocating, but it is known that in the creation of the park hundreds of mountain families were forced to leave their homes (the official estimate is over twelve hundred people). Most national parks before that time were formed from lands already owned by the federal government and, apart from some mining and ranching, largely undeveloped and unpopulated. Yellowstone, established in 1872, was the first to be created, followed by others, including Yosemite (1890), Mount Rainier (1899), Crater Lake (1902), Wind Cave (1903), Denali (1917), and Grand Canyon (1919). However, the land that was to become the Great Smoky Mountains National Park was neither remote nor unpopulated. Nor was it owned by the federal government, but by private owners in more than sixty-six hundred separate parcels. Most of the land belonged to timber and pulpwood companies, but the rest comprised farms and homes.

The promoters of the park faced a financial problem of raising the money to buy the land, and a PR problem of persuading the American people that this was for the public good. John D. Rockefeller Jr. came to the financial rescue, donating $5 million to add to other private donations and the federal government's $2 million. Public support was harder to win, and came through a vigorous propaganda campaign that highlighted the beauty of the land and its potential for tourism as well as the damage done by the logging industry and the need to protect the environment. It also employed negative stereotypes of the mountain dwellers to justify their removal from the park. The knowledge that the mountain people had been portrayed as uncivilized and bestial put Dolly's representation of them in her songs as like birds and animals in a different light for me. Dolly's romantic imagery can be seen as a subversion of these slurs and stereotypes. She too uses images from the natural world (women are often flowers or birds, men wild winds), but to enhance rather than demean mountain people. In 2009, Dolly performed at the celebrations to mark the seventy-fifth anniversary of the dedication of the park, but it is an irony that the original establishment of the national park, the Smoky Mountain paradise that her songs eulogize as "home," had in fact made her predecessors homeless.

We walked for a while into the forest, where the insistent verticality of the trees induced a kind of vertigo even when the ground was not particularly elevated. It was undeniably beautiful, especially in the changing light, but if I am honest I prefer my nature in a Dolly Parton song or Ansel Adams photograph. The reality of a thickness of trees is too Hansel and Gretel, or *Blair Witch Project*. So we soon left in pursuit of Dolly Parton's childhood home in Locust Ridge. According to the map, Locust Ridge was northeast of Gatlinburg and southeast of Sevierville, just beyond the northernmost boundary of the national park. However, neither the fold-up map nor the pages printed off from Google Maps made me confident about finding it. The fold-up map did not have Locust Ridge marked at all. The green indicator on Google Maps appeared to have been planted in the middle of nowhere, like a cartographic version of Pin the Tail on the Donkey. It was on Locust Ridge Road, but what exactly "it" was—a house, a collection of houses and stores—was unclear. The only guidance I had as to what we were looking for was the photograph of the house on the cover of the album, *My Tennessee Mountain Home*. Deciding that local knowledge would be an asset, we drove the short distance to Sevierville, a city whose major thoroughfare, Dolly Parton Parkway, shows its pride in its hometown girl star.

We parked the car on Court Avenue, grabbed a soda, and approached the courthouse, a building of disordered design, with a white Italianate clock tower studded with gold domes atop a red brick base with Romanesque windows. "Faux baroque" was Tony's description. The courthouse says "look at me" as if trying to make up for the lack of panache in nondescript downtown Sevierville. On the lawn in front of the courthouse are two memorials. On the left, as you face the building, stands a monument crowned by a fearsome eagle and dedicated to Sevier County veterans. On the right, in contrast to military solemnity, is a bronze statue of Dolly Parton, girlish, barefoot, and with crossed legs, strumming her guitar (fig. 18). Sevierville honored Dolly with the statue, sculpted by a local artist, Jim Gray, and unveiled by Dolly herself in 1987. She has said that having a statue erected by the people who knew her, folks from the place where she was born, is the thing she is most proud of. It is a sunny statue, capturing the singer's optimism. However, it had not been cleaned in a while, and I felt moved to brush away cobwebs that were suspended between the statue's legs. It would have felt wrong to leave them there, but it was a strangely intimate gesture that made me feel uncomfortable all the same.

18. The statue of Dolly Parton outside the Sevierville Courthouse

Inside the courthouse, the women seated behind windows were happy to help give directions to Locust Ridge, but none could be sure where it was. So we had no choice but to follow the directions given by Google Maps, which were as follows: get onto the Dolly Parton Parkway, turn right onto TN-416S, turn left toward Richardson Cove Road, turn right onto Richardson Cove Road, continue onto Locust Ridge Road, turn left to stay on Locust Ridge Road, slight right to stay on Locust Ridge Road, turn right to stay on Locust Ridge Road, Locust Ridge. Whether we failed to find Locust Ridge, or whether we found it but didn't recognize it, I don't know. The landscape around Locust Ridge Road (which proved harder to stay on than a road should) became increasingly rural. There were fields and shacks and cabins, and I realized that without signposting I wouldn't recognize the old Parton house anyway. The more wooden structures we saw, some in use, some abandoned, and the more Tony had to swerve to avoid mailboxes as the road became a narrow dirt track, the more I wondered what on earth we were doing. It seemed quite ludicrous to be driving deeper and deeper into the kind of countryside that Scully and Mulder used to visit when investigating some paranormal horror. It also seemed prurient. If Dolly Parton's childhood home was still out there, not signposted, then who were we to ferret it out?

Perhaps the original house no longer exists. In any case, its mythic status for Dolly Parton fans gives it an imaginary power that is greater than any physical reality. More than one simulation of the house exists. Famously, Dolly has a replica of the house on show at Dollywood that we were to see when we visited the theme park the following day. It is also rumored that Dolly's Nashville home has parts of her childhood house built into it. Cecelia Tichi uses the term "reliquary" to describe this, meaning that the new home contains parts of the old like a medieval reliquary would contain the remains or relics of a saint. Lest this seem a far-fetched image, some of Dolly Parton's most dedicated admirers do behave like worshippers of saints. In 2008 a documentary film about Dolly's followers was made, called *For the Love of Dolly*, offering what the blurb on the back of the DVD describes as "a poignant and heartfelt look at some of her most avid fans." The film's tagline is "Dolly Parton is more than a country singer. She is a way of life." I didn't see the film until after I'd returned from my journey (I bought it in the Dixie Stampede gift shop), but watching it made me realize that compared to Dolly's superfans I was a pathetic excuse for an admirer.

Take Jeanette, who has built a replica of Dolly's childhood home in the garden of her parents' house in California. More accurately, she has built a replica of the replica, confessing in the film that she had broken off a piece of wood from the cabin at Dollywood ("to take to Home Depot" to match the color and texture exactly). She has incorporated into the floor of her cabin Dolly Parton's signature and the title of a song that she asked Dolly to write out for her. From one perspective this seems a bit mad, but from another it is entirely consonant with the tacit contract between idol and fan. In another scene in the film we are shown Dolly giving away rocks from her childhood home to fans at Dollywood. The rocks are treated here like saints' relics; they have a talismanic power. It may be that Dolly's childhood home will provide for the world as many rocks and pieces of wood as Saint Thomas has his bones, and Saint Theresa her robes . . .

Jeanette explains the reverence she has for Dolly and anything associated with Dolly. "Anything she touches, I mean, we want. . . . You don't launder it: it's history. You retire it." Jeanette has "retired" the boots, shirt, and underwear that she was wearing the first time she met Dolly. She has kept a bead that fell off one of her costumes. In the most extraordinary scene in the film, Jeanette and her flatmate Melisa, another Dolly Parton fan, spot a car in a car dealership that they recognize belonged to Judy Ogle, Dolly's long-time friend and personal assistant. It looks as if the car has been traded in, and Jeanette and Melisa go and examine it. They are beside themselves with excitement when they find a Tennessee insurance card inside the vehicle made out to Judy Ogle and Dolly Parton that seems to confirm their detective work. Jeanette, part serious, part hamming it up for the camera, sniffs and licks the seat belts. She picks up a hair from the floor. "Oh my god!" she shrieks, "One with a root!'

The film exposes the extremes to which some people structure their lives (time, money, fantasy) around Dolly Parton, and how a celebrity is treated like saints used to be, but Tai Uhlmann, the director, does not ridicule her subjects. One of the questions she poses is why some people are attracted to having this kind of relationship with a famous person. One answer is that for those who don't have nurturing families, Dolly becomes a substitute. To some of her fans, Dolly Parton herself has become home. Melisa, estranged from her family because of childhood abuse issues, explains: "Most people would think, well, what would my mom say, or you'd call your mom and say, 'Hey, this is happening. What should I do?' I don't have that. So, for me, I can't call Dolly, but I can pretend. I can think OK, I've heard her say this before, or 'I know this,' or you know, in her book she says this . . . and that's just how I guided myself through my childhood and my early adulthood and got me to this point, you know. And I think I'm sort of a sane person because of it." She certainly comes across as sane, strong, and likeable. Dolly Parton played a role in her imaginative life from when Melisa was a child. She admits: "I used to pretend I was adopted and that secretly Dolly was my mom." This may be a more common fantasy than many realize. It is the subject of Tara Johns's 2011 film *The Year Dolly Parton Was My Mom*, an independent Canadian film set in 1976 that focuses on a teenager who learns that she is adopted and becomes convinced that Dolly Parton must be her biological mother.

One thing that struck me, listening to Melisa, with whom I have much in common even if I have never shared her specific fantasy, is how, well, *sensible* she is about her extreme fandom. She is self-aware and matter-of-fact: "My own little fantasy of her got me through so much. I needed sort of a positive guidance and I found that in Dolly." At the end of the documentary we are told that Melisa decided to take time off from following Dolly to focus on a career and that she has moved from Nashville. I think about her sometimes and truly hope she is doing well. One anecdote Melisa tells about her life as a devoted fan of the singer shows why Dolly Parton is the perfect fantasy mother. Melisa relates that one of her childhood prayers was that every night "Dolly would tuck me in and say goodnight to me so that I could feel safe at night." When the adult Melisa and her friend Jeanette were camping out every night on the set of Dolly's film *Unlikely Angel*, Dolly chatted with them and Melisa told her about this childhood fantasy. And every night before she went to bed, Dolly Parton came out of her trailer, went over to the two figures huddled in sleeping bags, and wished Melisa goodnight. Angel indeed.

6

Color Me America

Dollywood is not the only entertainment co-owned by, operated by, and identified with Dolly Parton. Near the amusement park, on the Parkway in Pigeon Forge, is "Dolly Parton's Dixie Stampede Dinner Attraction: The Smokies' Most Fun Place to Eat!" The Dixie Stampede first opened in 1988, has a sister show in Branson, Missouri, and used to have another in Orlando, Florida (2003–2008, now closed), and another in Myrtle Beach, South Carolina (1992–2010, replaced by "Pirates Voyage" with a musical score by Dolly Parton). With only a dim notion of what a "dinner attraction" might involve, Tony, Athena and I arrived at the Dixie Stampede building, whose "Wild West" exterior was a gentle foretaste of the evening ahead.

We were early and killed time examining an exhibit in the lobby dedicated to Dolly Parton's Imagination Library, an initiative to encourage children to read by partnering with local resources to mail a new and specially selected book to every preschool child once a month (fig. 19). Part of the exhibit is a large model of an open book, whose page on the left-hand side is characteristically aspirational: "Dolly's gift to Sevier County preschool children and message to the world to Dream More . . . Learn More . . . Care More . . . Be More." The opposite page explains the philosophy behind the project with an acrostic:

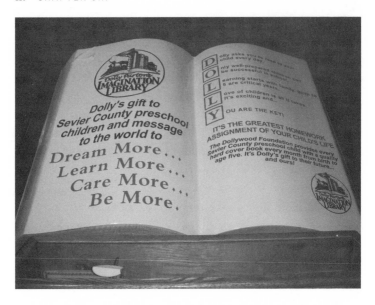

19. Dolly Parton's Imagination Library display at the Dixie Stampede

Dolly asks you to read to your child every day
Only well prepared children can be successful at school
Learning starts with Family. Birth to 5 are critical years.
Love of children is all it takes. It's exciting and . . .
YOU ARE THE KEY!

We read about how Dolly started the program because "she wanted children to be excited about books and to feel the magic that books can create" and so that "she could ensure that every child would have books, regardless of their family's income." Even Tony, who had sniffed at the sentimentality of the children's book *I Am a Rainbow* written by Dolly Parton, a book that talks about emotions and whose concluding lines he quotes to me annoyingly whenever I am sour-tempered ("So be a rainbow—shine above and filter all your glow through love"), even Tony was impressed by the Imagination Library. The project began on a small scale in 1996 and served the children of Sevier County. Today the Imagination Library has over 600,000 children registered in the United States, Canada, and England. It has distributed over forty million books for free and in 2000 was honored by the Association of American Publishers for its promotion of books and authors. Dolly has said that being called "the book lady" was the achievement of hers of which her father was most proud.

The book display is a bit incongruous in the lobby of the Dixie Stampede, which is otherwise themed as a wooden "carriage room" decorated with horse paraphernalia. At an appointed time, about an hour and a half before the start of the main show, we were ushered through (via a compulsory photograph opportunity, where our pictures were taken against olde worlde backgrounds: a gristmill, a country stream) to a "pre-show experience" in a saloon-style dining room. Waitresses dressed like extras from *Gone with the Wind* served us nonalcoholic cocktails in souvenir Dixie Stampede plastic cups that were shaped like cowboy boots. Athena was delighted. I asked our server if she enjoyed working for the Dixie Stampede. She told me that she loved the job, except when the feathers in her hat wouldn't stand up straight. She was saving up to study at the University of Nashville and had not met Dolly Parton but that she treats her employees "real good," and smiled and added, "and this is fun!" And it was. The setting may have been knowingly tacky, but the bluegrass music played on the banjo, harmonica, violin, and guitar was fabulous, and all three of us were soon singing along and clapping with the rest to new songs, as well as old standards like "O, Susanna." The "pre-show" is optional, and on the evening we went it was only attended by a small group of people, but I highly recommend it for getting you in the right mood for the show to follow.

The brochure for Dixie Stampede emphasizes that the event is intimately associated with Dolly Parton, recreating the atmosphere of her childhood family get-togethers. Next to a photograph of a beaming Dolly in a red, white, and blue-sequined dress is the text: "When I was a little girl, my family would get together for some friendly competition. We'd laugh, yell, sing and then sit down to a huge meal. Dixie Stampede brings back those good old times." This suggests a close, if boisterous, gathering, but the brochure also boasted horses, acrobatics, and a "thunderous stampede" of cattle or buffalo. I asked the lady at the ticket booth how many seats were in the theater. "We can seat nineteen hundred," she said, "and I'm glad you prebooked, because we are already sold out for tonight." Nineteen hundred people numbers over a third of the population of Pigeon Forge; Dixie Stampede may market itself as a kind of souped-up family game night, but in reality it is a major operation.

The publicity material talks about "pitting North and South in a friendly and fun rivalry," but what we get is a friendly and fun version of the Civil War. That is a very odd sentence to write. It was even odder to experience. The show is performed in a stadium surrounded by rows of wooden benches, with a stage at one end whose backdrop displayed the image of a grand antebellum plantation house, much like Loretta Lynn's mansion in Hurricane Mills. The emcee informed us that we were to participate in the age-old battle between the North and the South and our "weapons" were to be clapping, shouting, and stamping our feet hard on the wooden floors to create the sounds of a stampede. What's that? A STAM—PEDE! Our teams of soldiers entered on horseback, the North to the tune of "Yankee Doodle" and the South to the tune of "Dixie's Land." Some members of the audience sang along to the music. (The words to "Dixie's Land" in the majority of its many versions do not merit close attention; there is a reason it is often referred to as the unofficial anthem of the Confederate states during the Civil War.) Others just yelled and cheered. We were on the side of the North, which at least made it easier to join in rooting for our team.

The North side was given blue flags to wave and the South gray, the colors of the Union and Confederate armies. The conflict itself was not restaged with significant historical realism, but it was given some sort of historical context. We were taken back through time to the early history of North America until the time when North and South went to war. On the level of spectacle much of this was simply thrilling. There was an acrobatic display worthy of the Cirque du Soleil, in which performers dressed as Cherokee Indians danced from the ceiling suspended by ribbons. The Indians, we were told, were the first inhabitants of North America and were spiritual people. This was followed by a train of covered wagons pulled by horses, with pioneers who sang, danced, and lassoed. The voice-over assured us that "with the settling of the West, America as we know it was born and the spirit of freedom began to grow." I tried to get my head round quite what had been glossed over here, massacres and displacements, for example, but I was distracted by the fire-eating. The North and South sides then competed with each other through pig racing (with and without hurdles), lumberjack competitions (Scotty "Redwood" Thompson climbed, sawed, and chopped for the team), and trials involving selected members of the audience, barrels, and toilet seats. I would never have anticipated the exhilaration of pig racing. It was brilliant fun. There was no slavery, sectionalism, or territorial crisis to spoil the excitement of the North side and the South side seeing who could do the most impressive Mexican wave or the loudest stampede.

Sometime during the antics of a rascally character named Skeeter and his dancing chicken, Nugget, servers costumed in military uniforms from the Civil War era distributed to each member of the audience a three-course meal to be eaten without cutlery: a bowl of vegetable soup and biscuit, a whole chicken, a slice of ham, a baked potato, buttered corn on the cob, and an iced apple pastry. The food was fantastic, but the sight of nearly two thousand whole chickens being ripped apart while in the arena below a man in a chicken costume did a jig, Skeeter cracked mother-in-law jokes, and horses jumped through hoops of fire, was very strange indeed.

No modern parallel does the Dixie Stampede justice, neither the circus nor Vaudeville. It is however, reminiscent of the ancient Roman arena, where political theater was similarly couched as entertainment involving displays of exotic animals, feats of human endurance, and re-enactments of famous wars. The Roman spectacles were bloodier and more expensive. In the *naumachia*, the staged sea battle, the arena was flooded, allowing prisoners of war and condemned criminals to replay the battles of Salamis (originally fought between Greeks and Persians in 480 BCE), of Corcyra and Corinth (two Greek states who came to blows in 434 BCE), and of Actium (the decisive conflict in 31 BCE in the Roman Civil War, in which Augustus beat Mark Antony and Cleopatra). Historians usually assume that the Roman re-enactments must have been choreographed so that the winning sides won all over again, especially in the case of Augustus's staging of the battle of Actium, a theatrical repeat of his own martial victory. However, the Dixie Stampede made me rethink this. Who won and who lost in the Dixie Stampede conflict was far less important than the ideological theater that preceded the announcement of victory. The night that we attended the North won, a result that did nothing to upset the historical record. However, in a real sense the South won, and the tallying of points and declaration of a winner were irrelevant. The whole evening is a celebration of the South. In an essay in 1945 entitled "A Northerner Views the South" cultural anthropologist Ruth Landes wrote that in the images created by popular culture the South was "gilded in sentimentality." It is a phrase that perfectly sums up the South of the Dixie Stampede, with its chivalrous gentleman, glamorous ladies, and mint julep–scented tableaus. At one point the voice-over said something like "The North has given us lots of great things like the Statue of Liberty, but the South . . ." and

the lights faded while a glittering pagoda was lowered from
the ceiling, containing southern belles twirling parasols and
wearing hooped skirts in jewel colors that sparkled with tiny
lights. There was a collective gasp at the beauty of the spectacle. In the Dixie Stampede, the South always wins.
This is where the Dixie Stampede has its (iced) cake and
eats it. For before the audience could reflect upon the result
of their civil conflict, the grand finale erupted in a crescendo
of patriotism. Horses cantered in formation with their riders
wearing lighted costumes of red, white, and blue and waving the American flag. "Are you proud to be an American?"
boomed the emcee. A supersized image of a resplendent red,
white, and blue Dolly Parton that fills the entire screen at the
end of the stadium responded: "No North, no South, no East,
no West—but one *United* States of America! Freedom and
justice for all!!" Dolly is here! Dolly is a *dea ex machina* who will
make America well!!! Dolly IS America!!!! The crowd erupts,
screaming, clapping, and stamping. On screen Dolly starts to
sing her song "Color Me America, Red, White and Blue" and
a now impassioned and teary crowd stand and join in as the
verses segue into those of "America the Beautiful."

After the ovation we were funneled out along a corridor
hung with large photographs of Dolly thanking us and bid-
ding us to come back soon, and emerged, blinking, into the
anticlimax of the gift shop. The gift shop was packed with
Dolly souvenirs, from packets of the Dixie Stampede creamy
vegetable soup, to the Dixie Stampede official horse orna-
ment, called "American Spirit." It seemed to me that how Dolly
Parton is marketed to her local audience has a rather different
emphasis from how she is marketed to her international audience. Locally, the Christian and patriotic Dolly are strongly
promoted with, for example, a large display of her CD *For God
and Country*, and not a photo of Dolly with Boy George or a
copy of *Transamerica* in sight.

I bought a copy of *For God and Country* and listened to it

back at the hotel. Released in 2003, it rode a wave of patriotism in country music after the attacks on America on September 11, 2001. In some ways the album is recognizably Dolly Parton, with several tracks about coming home, and a couple about hope for a new beginning. However, it is uncharacteristic of her work in its lack of irony and self-parody. There are light touches, as in the arrangement of a verse in the traditional song "When Johnny Comes Marching Home," which has been doctored to recognize the women in the armed forces as well as the men ("When Janey comes marching home . . . 'cause Janey too has done her best, she's fought as hard as all the rest"), but most of the album is a serious slab of Christian patriotism, from the first track ("The Lord Is My Shepherd") to the last ("The Glory Forever"). It also contains some of Dolly Parton's most explicitly political material, as with the following voice-over: "Oh, the mother of all battles is what Saddam had planned. Well, he shoulda sent his mother 'cause his troops all turned and ran." There may not be much irony in the album, but there is some to its anti-Saddam Hussein stance. In 2002, a year before both the US-led bombing of Iraq and the release of *For God and Country*, Saddam Hussein ran for re-election. His campaign adopted as its theme song an Arabic cover version of Dolly Parton's *I Will Always Love You*, sung by Syrian pop star Mayyada Bselees. I have been unable to track down the footage used in the TV commercials that reportedly shows Saddam kissing babies and posing with guns, underscored by the song, but an MP3 file of the music is available on the Internet. The Mayyada Bselees version sounds, to my ears at least, more plangent than the Dolly Parton original or Whitney Houston version, more a question than a statement of conviction: *I Will Always Love You?*

Later that evening I was upset and upset at being upset. In Nashville, reading the letter of Gerald Ford in the Country Music Hall of Fame and Museum, I had taken on board that to think about country music was to think about America. However, I had not reckoned on being confronted so directly with America, American history, and American values as I was in the Dixie Stampede. Nor had I anticipated feeling less close, an aversion even, to Dolly Parton, as a result. It was the dishonest history that was most troubling: the censorship of any aspects of American history (what happened to the Cherokee Indians, slavery) that might tarnish the image of the USA as embodying "justice for us all," as *Color Me America* puts it. Coming to the Dixie Stampede so soon after seeing some of the sanitized histories of the South, the lionization of Nathan Bedford Forrest, and the gloss on slavery by the sign marking the Midway Plantation Slave Cemetery, made it impossible not to view the Dixie Stampede through a culturally sensitive lens. However, that evening I wanted very strongly to be able to switch off my critical self, and felt highly anxious about judging Dolly Parton negatively. It amounted to a kind of heresy, I thought, and I was unprepared, in retrospect naively, for the feeling of alienation from the woman I had so long admired.

"This is your *The Wizard of Oz* moment," said Tony, not unkindly. That gave me pause. *The Wizard of Oz*, a master narrative of the questing journey, not only tells us that there will be disenchantment with the object of the quest, disenchantment perhaps built into any relationship that is based on idealization, but also stresses that what the seeker is really looking for is to be found in herself. Indeed, it is a cliché of the pilgrimage that it fundamentally involves the universal quest for the self. This all seemed too cute a story for me: I had come to get to know Dolly Parton, not myself. However, a few months later I read an interview (with Michael Joseph Gross) in which Dolly comments on what she thinks her admirers are often looking for when they come to see her, and it made me think again about that tortured evening in Pigeon Forge: "A lot of times my fans don't come to see me be me. They come to see me be them. They come to hear me say what they want to hear, what they'd like to say themselves, or to say about them what they believe is true." If this is true, and my response to the Dixie Stampede would seem to confirm it, then is pilgrimage really a search for self-knowledge, or is it rather an exercise in narcissism?

7

Sifting Specks of Gold

Dollywood is, to my knowledge, the only amusement park in the world to be themed around a woman. There are plenty of parks themed around men. We have a choice of Bobbejaanland, first established and run in the 1960s by the late Flemish singer and guitarist Bobbejaan Schoepen in Lichtaart, Belgium; or the Bruce Lee Memorial Park in honor of the martial arts expert and actor, in Shunde, Southern China; or maybe Dickens World, themed around the life and works of Charles Dickens (and where children can romp happily in Fagin's Den), in Kent, England. Few have not visited, let alone not heard of, one of the amusement parks created around Walt Disney and the characters in his films: Disneyland in California, Walt Disney World in Florida, Disneyland Paris, and Tokyo Disneyland in Chiba, Japan, parks that have set the gold standard for family theme park entertainment. Or, for those who prefer their men fictional, you may enjoy Parc Astérix near Paris and the Wizarding World of Harry Potter in Orlando, Florida. But as yet there is no Detecting World of Nancy Drew, Oprahville, or Austenland. There is, however, Dollywood.

Dollywood distracts from its radical status with clusters of butterflies on its welcoming placards, images of its namesake smiling beatifically, and posters bearing the park's twenty-fifth-anniversary motto, "Celebrate the Dreamer in You" (fig.

20. Butterflies, real and inflatable, are everywhere at Dollywood.

20). These symbolic enticements also draw the visitor's attention away from the park's utilitarian aspects, from the trolleys
that pick up visitors at the many parking lots far away from the
park itself and transport them to the entrance, and from the
pedestrian business of buying tickets and shuffling through
turnstiles. Despite the anxieties of the previous evening I was
atremble with excitement and determined to accentuate the
positive. Overwrought with the anticipation of pleasures to
come, we sat down on a bench a little way inside the park to
study the map. The minute we had done so, Dolly Parton's
tinkling voice rang out in greeting, "Hello there!" and for an
unnerving instant we turned around trying to work out where
she was and whether it was really her, before the voice continued speaking and we realized that we must have triggered a
hidden sensor. "Let me share with you one of my silver memories," said the disembodied voice of Dolly before it sang a sad
song about a man called John Daniel, who had calloused hands

(I couldn't catch the rest of it) and reminded us to "Celebrate the Dreamer in You!" It was one of the many surreal moments designed to impress upon you that you are in Dolly's space, and that she is always close by with a song or a kind word. It encourages a hypervigilance, an alertness to who or what may next surprise you, an attitude encouraged by tales that Dolly Parton often visits the park, and even (a disputed rumor) that she has a home on the grounds.

The map showed that the park is arranged with the majority of its attractions in one long strip at its base, from which protrudes a long loop of rides, shops, and restaurants surrounding and surrounded by forests of trees. We were in a world that was strikingly artificial and stimulating, but at the same time just as impressively within the Smoky Mountains, with all of their natural beauty and calm. It was a very different sensory experience from anything I had ever encountered before. Dollywood has its own temporal and spatial dynamics that were recognizable but nonetheless askew from those in everyday life. Neither yesterday nor tomorrow mattered, only there and then. It was like a 3-D version of a virtual-reality world. It even has its own currency, Dolly Dollars (of course!), as if to underline that it is a world apart.

I am ashamed to say that into this otherworldly loveliness intruded some all too mundane observations. Such as, I have never seen so many fat people together in one place. So many unrepentant fat people, dressed in capri pants and sleeveless tops. It was as if Dollywood had been specially prepared for Jamie Oliver to fly in and start berating people about the importance of fresh vegetables. I did not observe this from the perspective of a slender critic; I fitted right in. I grew up in Eastbourne, reputedly the town with the largest population of fat people in England. It should be twinned with Pigeon Forge. I am even more ashamed to admit that, in part because we were flummoxed by the overwhelming number of choices we could make, the number of things to do and see, and in part to combat the heat with liquid and the excitement with carbs, the first thing we did was go somewhere called the Lumber Camp and slug sodas and eat fried banana pudding with squirty cream and caramel sauce. If one of the purposes of pilgrimage is purification and regeneration, on the physical front at least, I failed miserably.

Dollywood is themed in three major ways: around Dolly Parton's life story, around local geography and tradition, and around American symbols and values. As these also feature prominently in her songs, the visitor who is familiar with her music gains a whole extra dimension to the park. Dollywood is a virtual world that gives physical form to many of Dolly's songs. The chapel is named after Dr. Robert F. Thomas, the doctor who delivered Dolly as a baby, and about whom, as I've previously noted, she wrote a song. The song "Applejack" is represented by Applejack's restaurant. The Eagle Foundation is not just a symbol of America, but also evokes "Eagle When She Flies," and the butterflies that inhabit the park, both real and painted, are reminders that "Love Is Like a Butterfly." The park's recurring motto "Celebrate the Dreamer in You" reflects the lyrics of the inspirational "Light of a Clear Blue Morning": "I got my dreams to see me through," and the green leaves and rippling water of the streams and foliage in Dollywood reflect those depicted in the video to that song. The physical attractions triggered an inaudible soundtrack that played in snatched refrains in my head. Seeing the Friendship Fountain cued "Everything's Beautiful in Its Own Way" ("When I see a fountain flow from a mountain . . ."); pausing to enjoy a blue-grass band in a shaded bandstand on an incline sparked a burst of indignation from "Star of the Show" ("I don't play second fiddle in nobody's band. And I'm no backup singer and I won't be a fan"). Dollywood is a world in which everything seems potentially meaningful, an allusion to Dolly's life, lyrics, or values that should not be missed.

Several of Dolly's songs have no place in the park. These

paint a grim and unsentimental portrait of family life, one in which poverty is not ennobling and parents and spouses (usually the men) let down their loved ones. Songs like "Mommie, Ain't That Daddy" and "Daddy's Moonshine Still" attest to the damage inflicted by alcoholism and bootlegging, with women driven to despair and prostitution. In "Daddy, Come and Get Me," a woman has been put into a mental institution because her lover wants her out of the way. Dollywood is unsurprisingly selective about its references and allusions: this is good, clean, family fun.

Central to the presentation of Dolly's biography in the park is the Chasing Rainbows Museum, located in an area called Adventures in Imagination. The beginning of the tour seemed rather familiar. Just inside the entrance was a whiteboard with a handwritten message: "Hey, Judy, Look at the photo vault for 9 to 5 pictures. I need to send some to Jane. Dolly." I asked a friendly staff member for an interpretation and was told that Jane is the person in charge of the museum and that Dolly leaves messages for people here to show her "personal touch." Further inside were more handwritten messages interspersed with photographs of Dolly Parton with other celebrities, including Julie Andrews, Oprah Winfrey, Carol Burnett, Miss Piggy, the Judds, Barbra Streisand, Grace Jones, Tanya Tucker and daughter Presley, Frank Sinatra, Boy George, Johnny Cash, and Jimmy Carter and his wife Rosalynn. Some of these notes were straightforward ("Sis, do they have any more of these cheap frames at the mall or at the dime store?") and others enigmatic ("Call Regis and ask him for my million bucks"), which strengthened the impression of being a special invitee into Dolly's personal space. However, seeing this so soon after seeing the same technique in Loretta Lynn's museum in Hurricane Mills made it seem more of a motif than a genuinely personal touch. It would be interesting to know who borrowed the idea from whom (and whether either of them feels ripped off).

More of a delight is Dolly's Attic, an old-fashioned *Wun-*

derkammer, or "wonder room." It is a captivating cabinet of curiosities and sentimental items from Dolly Parton's childhood and working life. I began to examine a cross-stitch sampler made by Dolly's mother Avie Lee Parton, with all of her children's names and birth dates, when the far wall lit up and a life-size Dolly was projected onto it, singing "I've Been Chasing Rainbows." She then smiles and says, "Boo! I hope that scared you as much as it scared me!" Well, yes. Athena and I were alone in the attic when she appeared and, like the surprise audio track, the effect is uncanny. Phantasm Dolly proceeds to describe some of the objects in her attic—Carl Dean's favorite chair, an old machine for removing cellulite—and explains, "I save everything. I think that comes from growing up poor." She imparts some homespun wisdom that feels especially apt for those, like us, who have come far to see her: "I think this life is not a destination in itself but a journey, and the most important part of this journey is how you travel, and I hope you get something real special out of your journey here today." This may sound hokey now, but at the time the sincerity of Phantasm Dolly was quite compelling. Her final words made clear the inspirational agenda of Dollywood: "You might have to flip off a few specks of dust—dust of experience, risk, and reward, and above all else love. Maybe from my life's dust you can sift a few specks of gold to help you on your life's journey."

Walt Disney was also explicit about his agenda for Disneyland in a speech he delivered at the opening of the park in 1955. The speech is inscribed on a plaque in front of the statue of Disney in the park, and the relevant part of it reads: "Disneyland is dedicated to the ideals, the dreams, and the hard facts that have created America . . . with the hope that it will be a source of joy and inspiration to all the world." Dollywood, like Disneyland, envisages itself as a source of inspiration, but Dollywood ties the source of this inspiration more closely to its founder and namesake than Disneyland does. Dolly Parton is set up as a model to inspire and help her park's visitors live better lives. The DVD "insider's tour" of the Chasing Rainbows Museum reinforces this message with a different metaphor: "I have chased many rainbows from my Tennessee Mountain home as a little girl . . . to Nashville . . . to Hollywood . . . and all around the world. I have been truly blessed with a voice and a passion to create music, and I hope that sharing some of my good fortune will in some way inspire you to chase your own personal rainbow." The biography of Dolly Parton lends itself to the physical design of the park, with gift shops like Cas Walker's Store, named after the music impresario on whose Knoxville TV show Dolly was a regular from the age of ten. But more than that, as the Chasing Rainbows Museum demonstrates, Dolly's life story also shapes the moral and emotional climates of Dollywood.

The museum and the park as a whole hit hard the "rags to riches" arc of Dolly's biography. In a green leafy area we found the cabin, Dolly's legendary Tennessee Mountain home, and peered through the glass wall into the two rooms that meticulously recreate the period, with a gas lamp on the kitchen table, curtains on the dresser that look as if they are made of sacking, and one room wallpapered with newspapers and catalogues (Hurricane Mills again!) (figs. 21 and 22). It was hard to imagine twelve children and their parents living in such a small space; no wonder they spent so much time outdoors. Perhaps the most poignant exhibit in Chasing Rainbows is the "coat of many colors," the coat made famous from Dolly's song that tells of a formative episode in her childhood when her mother, not being able to afford to buy her a new coat, stitched one together from different-colored rags and told her daughter the Bible story of Joseph and his coat of many colors. The other children at her school mocked her in her new coat, but even though the taunting upset her, Dolly knew that she was "as rich as I could be" because her mama had made the coat with love. The coat itself, and this is testament to Avie Lee Parton's skill as a seamstress as well as to the ironies of fashion,

21. Dolly Parton's childhood home reconstructed as a theme park attraction

looks as if it could have come from the Gap. The right-hand side is eggshell blue corduroy with a navy blue sleeve, and the left-hand side primrose yellow with a dark red sleeve. Blocks of the same colors are stitched around the bottom of the coat, and there's a single button holding it together beneath the collar. It is a beautiful coat. Standing bravely in its glass case along with some autumn leaves and the handwritten lyrics to its owner's song, positioned in front of a sepia photograph of children pointing and jeering on the wall behind, the exhibit powerfully conveys the young Dolly's vulnerability and maturity. The song about the coat is used as a source of reflection and pedagogical guide for children today. The Country Music Hall of Fame and Museum Teachers' Resource Guide recommends that teachers ask students to listen to "Coat of Many Colors" and then write a "reaction paper" considering various questions, including "Has someone ever made something spe-

22. The interior of the replica of Dolly's childhood home

cial for you? How did that make you feel?" and "Have you ever been part of a group that made fun of someone? Explain why you think people make fun of others."

The fairy tale of Cinderella, one classic narrative of the rags-to-riches life story, sprinkles its specks of gold over Dolly Parton and her work. The press have called her "America's modern-day Cinderella," and it is an association she has encouraged in her work and in the park. Her 1992 comedy *Straight Talk* is a variation on the Cinderella story, with Dolly as a simple country girl, Shirlee Kenyon. Through lucky breaks, natural talent, and the eventual rescue by James Woods as the newspaper editor-cum-Prince Charming, Kenyon ends up with her man and a job as a radio talk show host. Lest the parallels with the fairy tale be lost on an audience, one of the posters advertising the film has Dolly Parton's character perched on a pumpkin looking wistfully up at the midnight sky. One of the songs from the movie equates the "Cinderella fairy tale" with chasing "the all-American dream." The steam train that runs through Dollywood, taking its passengers on a ride through the Smoky Mountains, is named *Cinderella* (fig. 23). In this park every attention has been paid to theming and symbolism, and the name of the steam train is intended to be significant. The Chasing Rainbows Museum makes it clear that Dolly Parton has worked her own way out of poverty, not waited for someone to rescue her, and that her value comes from what she does as much as what she looks like. The biography of Dolly Parton is one of breaking through the hierarchy of social order, of moving up a social and economic class, no matter what protestations are made about remaining "a simple country girl." The biography of Cinderella, at least in the most well-known modern version of the tale in the 1950 animated film by Walt Disney, is one in which social and economic hierarchies are maintained and validated. Cinderella was born

23. Dollywood's steam locomotive, Cinderella

into a wealthy aristocratic family; she is in rags only because her mother has died and her stepmother and stepsisters abuse and deprive the young woman through jealousy of her beauty and charm (always innate qualities of the elite in Disney narratives). Casting Dolly Parton as Cinderella hides the fact that Dolly's transformation has been a social and economic one, as well as a personal one. It underplays the nature of her success.

As Dollywood is sometimes referred to as "an Appalachian Disneyland" or "the redneck Disneyland," it is worth comparing her fairy tale more closely to those promoted in the California amusement park. Athena and I went to Disneyland, our first ever visit, several months after our journey around Tennessee. We met Cinderella there (or rather a "cast member" impeccably made up as her), accompanied by some of the other Disney princesses, Snow White (the happy homemaker), Ariel (poster girl for giving up your voice to please a man), and Belle from *Beauty and the Beast* (accommodating wife of an abusive husband). We did not see Mulan, the defiant Chinese warrior, nor the feisty Merida from the movie *Brave*, which had not yet been released. We went on the Pirates of the Caribbean ride, Athena terrified of the dark, the mist, and the sudden dips, but determined to see her favorite character from the movies: Elizabeth Swann, and the pirates Anamaria and Angelica. Instead we saw a slave auction, "Take a Wench for a Bride," in which women in shackles were being hooted at by drunken animatronic pirates. The ride itself was created before the *Pirates of the Caribbean* movies were made, but Captains Jack Sparrow, Barbossa, and Blackbeard, three of the main male characters in the films, were later added to the ride. Elizabeth Swann, Anamaria, and Angelica, however, are omitted completely. Athena was so upset that it took two pineapple ices to calm her down.

Compared to this retrograde display of female roles, Dollywood offers more progressive models for a girl to identify with. In Dolly's fairy tale, it's no use waiting for a Prince

Charming; a girl has to make her own luck. In this she not only contrasts with the Disney princess, but with Loretta Lynn, whom, as we saw at Hurricane Mills, also casts herself as a Cinderella, but who credits her late husband with engineering her achievements. Dolly is both Cinderella *and* her fairy godmother, and she has no need for a Prince Charming. In Chasing Rainbows there are displays that celebrate Dolly Parton's relationships with her husband, Carl Dean, and her late former collaborator Porter Wagoner, but Dolly herself is depicted as creating and owning her success. Unlike the fairy tale Cinderella, Dolly gives back to her community: through the Imagination Library and through the park itself. Dolly is also depicted, again unlike Cinderella, as having close relationships with women, especially her mother, her aunt Dorothy Jo, and her friend from childhood and personal assistant, Judy Ogle.

The press coverage of Dolly Parton's private life attempts to punish her, or so it would seem, for not behaving more like the fairy-tale Cinderella. Her husband's low media profile, coupled with her lifelong friendship with Judy Ogle, has prompted the press repeatedly, critically, and voyeuristically to accuse the two women of being lesbian lovers, something Dolly Parton has denied. You could take much of this reporting and replace the names of Dolly Parton, Carl Dean, and Judy Ogle with those of Oprah Winfrey, Stedman Graham, and Gayle King; the "scandals" told about Dolly Parton and Oprah Winfrey are virtually identical. They both betray an underlying anxiety about the strong and successful businesswoman who does not present herself as dependent on a man. Such a woman, suggest the stories in the *Globe* and its like, must have some shameful secret whose exposure would take her down a peg or two. Yet to many women, part of the allure of Dolly Parton (and of Oprah Winfrey) is precisely that they are ambitious and brilliant, yet still care about their sisters (ugly or not). Why is there no *National Enquirer* exclusive giving us the scoop that one formula for a woman's success is to have a close and loyal female friend? That's a far more interesting, if less lurid, subtext to ponder.

★   ★   ★

As in Disneyland, geography is important in Dollywood; it is the second major way through which the park is themed. Disneyland is divided into discrete geographical zones that mix elements of fantasy and reality: Adventureland (evoking the jungles of Asia and Africa), Frontierland (themed around the pioneer days along the American frontier), Fantasyland (with Peter Pan, and Sleeping Beauty's castle), and Tomorrowland (a space-age, futuristic zone). A short walk from Toontown, which was previously a country and western area until that proved unpopular, is a recreation of a New Orleans square as it might have been in the nineteenth century. All of these zones are reached by walking down Main Street, USA, a facsimile of an early twentieth-century Midwest town. Disneyland is more like the old world's fairs that used to juxtapose different countries and cultures than Dollywood, which has a more limited geo-graphical focus. Dollywood has had several incarnations, first opening as Rebel Railroad in 1961, and changing to Goldrush Junction in 1970. In 1967 Herschend Family Entertainment Corporation purchased the park and renamed it Silver Dollar City, Tennessee. In 1986 Dolly Parton took on co-ownership and the park was rebranded Dollywood. Now it is organized into ten areas, most of which have attractions that involve the history and culture of southern Appalachia: Showstreet, Rivertown Junction, Craftsmen's Valley, the Village, the Country Fair, Timber Canyon, Jukebox Junction, Owen's Farm, Adventures in Imagination, and Wilderness Pass. In 1987 Dolly said of the newly opened park that she wanted to build a fantasy world somewhere in the mountains for everyone to share with her and that she wanted to show what her part of the country was really like, and how her people really lived. The park aims to meet these goals by fusing the fantasy and the everyday.

Even though it is obvious that an amusement park is a carefully structured and tightly controlled environment, there are large areas of Dollywood that feel wonderfully natural. Riding on the coal-fired train, eyes watering from the breeze and the steam, it was impossible not to appreciate the staggering beauty of the mountains, sheering the sky with shades of blue and gray. I am aware of the irony that the packaged nature of the amusement park was more pleasurable (for us) than the oppressive experience of unrelieved forest in the national park. Other parts of the park have an oneiric quality, where the gentle babbling of a stream, the shadow play of ferns in the sunlight, and the haphazard flitting of tiny yellow butterflies conspire to create a hypnotic dreamworld where time stands still and everything is cloaked in a balmy serenity. How is that possible in an amusement park? Just thinking about amusement parks makes me want to lie down: the endless waiting in line, the whining of toddlers, and the crush of the crowds. Yet Dollywood has little oases of tranquility where all of that melts away.

Nature at its less serene is represented by the park's roller coasters. The Tennessee Tornado, a seventy-mile-per-hour, triple-loop steel roller coaster, and Thunderhead, a fifty-five-mile-per-hour wooden roller coaster, were the star attractions. Geographical precision is important to the theming of these rides. Mountain Slidewinder, a high-speed water toboggan ride, is given the following pitch: it is "situated in an authentic Smoky Mountain setting. Your adventure begins as you climb through the actual mountain terrain on your way to boarding this water toboggan thriller." The mountain location provides a frisson even before the precipitous plunge into water. Appalachia, present and past, is characterized as thrillingly dangerous. Mystery Mine is a steel roller coaster with an eighty-five-foot vertical drop taking you on a journey through an abandoned coal mine. Daredevil Falls takes its riders through an abandoned logging camp where they must dodge bears and discarded lumber machinery. It climaxes in a waterfall with a sixty-foot drop. In Blazing Fury the riders become recruits helping tackle a rampaging fire that is threatening to destroy a town set in the 1880s. It is an indoor roller coaster that drops through water, and the teenage girls we saw stumble through the exit were soaked, dazed, and beside themselves with pleasure. Tony and I are too cowardly, or maybe just too old, to appreciate being terrified, so we opted for the Smoky Mountain River Rampage, on which we negotiated rapids and waterfalls while seated in a large rubber tire. "We survived!'" cheered Athena as we clambered out, our pants sticking to our legs and with our shoes squelching. Part of the thrill of the Dollywood experience lies in a feeling that you know to be false but that is exhilarating anyway, that you have just encountered a life-or-death situation and have escaped unscathed and pumped-up to face another one.

These rides need their consumers to be active participants in the stories that they tell, stories that present the natural world, and mountain life, as inherently unstable. However, the terrors of the rides are licensed and temporary, unlike the real hazards of nature, such as floods. Most of the time, that is. We should note the cautionary tale of the male model Fabio and Apollo's Chariot. Fabio was the celebrity guest at the opening of the new Apollo's Chariot roller coaster ride at Busch Gardens Williamsburg, an amusement park in James City County, Virginia, on March 27, 1999. The name of the ride refers to the ancient Greek and Roman sun god Apollo. (Ancient Greek religion, in which deities represented natural phenomena and had their own symbolic spaces, provides one of the earliest historical examples of theming.) "Modern Day Adonis vs. Ancient Day Sun God" was the promotional sound bite, a touch hubristically as it turned out. Who with a basic knowledge of ancient myth would not have backed Apollo? On the inaugural ride of the roller coaster a goose flew straight into Fabio's face. The impact bloodied the model's nose and killed the bird. It is an example of nature and culture conspiring to remind humans not to take their dangers too lightly.

★   ★   ★

Shopping is a less fraught activity than riding roller coasters, and like the other attractions, most of the shops are themed around Dolly Parton's life and the region in which she was raised. Temple's Warehouse and Dry Goods is actually a toy store but is named in homage to a store in Sevierville that used to be run by the Temples and was frequented by Dolly's father to buy feed for his livestock. Disneyland has been criticized for promoting economic growth based on consumption, rather than production, and, in this, for being a metaphor for America as a whole. Dollywood is not open to quite the same criticism. It is more contradictory: what it offers for consumption is production, or a version of production. Rather than simply selling goods fashioned from glass, iron, wood, slate, and leather, Dollywood shows them being fashioned by professional craftsmen. There is a blacksmith and foundry, a glassworks, slate works and leather works. What they sell is the spectacle of the goods being made (and the sounds and heat of iron being smelted and the smell of leather as it is cut) and then, largely, souvenirs. Some are useful, such as leather jackets and hats, and others more decorative, such as slate tiles painted with mountain scenes. At Valley Carriage Works, you can buy handmade wagons: surreys, farm wagons, and specialty carriages. It is one of the country's few remaining working carriage shops. Dollywood might therefore be seen as promoting economic growth based on the revival of production, or at least consumption grounded in a respect for production and craftsmanship.

Indeed, respect would appear to be a hallmark of Dollywood, which was created in part to honor the people Dolly Parton grew up with. A plaque on the wall of Chasing Rainbows announces this loud and clear:

Something that fills me with pride is DOLLYWOOD
We celebrate the spirit of
the people who made a life
for themselves in that
very stingy countryside.
These are my real people.
The seed from which I sprang.
I saw DOLLYWOOD *as a chance to honor them!*

I found little to contradict this among the workers in the park. Whether meticulously scripted or heartfelt, everyone I spoke to professed their gratitude to Dolly Parton and their love of their jobs. It must help that workers at Dollywood are allowed to be versions of themselves, and from what I saw no one is made to dress up in humiliating *Hee Haw*–style costumes. I remember a moment in Disney California Adventure Park when we were dining in Ariel's Grotto and visited by a relay of Disney princesses. When Snow White came up to our table I said to her, "Poor Snow White, you must be fed up with smiling." She replied in character, "Oh no! I *love* smiling," but there was something strained in her eyes, as if she might snap at any moment and pull out an AK-47 from under her petticoats. There was no strain in the eyes of anyone I spoke to at Dollywood; the affection for Dolly Parton seemed widespread and genuine.

Dollywood is a concrete realization of the fantasy dramatized in Dolly's 2012 movie, *Joyful Noise*, in which the dreams and determination of a few country people, led by Dolly Parton's character, G. G. Sparrow, bring hope and cheer to their economically depressed community. It is also a shining example of beneficent capitalism, if that is not a contradiction in terms, and a letter from Ronald Reagan dated April 29, 1988, and displayed in the Chasing Rainbows Museum does not lose the opportunity to slip in a plug for "trickle down" economics: "Determination and concern like yours show how much private citizens can accomplish in meeting the needs of their communities." Dolly Parton herself avoids engaging in party politics, no doubt lest she alienate some of her audience. However, Dollywood, like the Dixie Stampede, is much occupied with American symbols and values.

The most visually impressive of these is the American Eagle Foundation, a thirty-thousand-square-foot aviary that houses the country's largest number of what they call "nonreleasable" bald eagles. Part conservation initiative, part spectacle, the American Eagle Foundation is "dedicated to protect the majestic Bald Eagle, the USA's National Symbol." Seen up close, in crabbed repose rather than gracious flight, the birds we looked at were rather menacing, still, and raptor-like and all too reminiscent of the eagle that I had encountered while in line to get my visa: Theodore Roszak's sinister gilded bird, poised on top of the American Embassy London Chancery Building, with its thirty-five-foot wingspan, as if about to swoop upon suspected illegal immigrants. A different kind of terror was in preparation at Dollywood: the construction of a new roller coaster in the Wilderness Pass area called the Wild Eagle, America's first ever steel-wing roller coaster. What that means is that the seats are alongside the central track, like wings, and there is no track below or above you as you hurtle through the air. Dolly Parton opened the ride on March 23, 2012, and gave an introductory speech that fused the eagle symbol and American values with the physical experience of riding the roller coaster: "I think that it represents the American spirit, just the human spirit. We all want to soar higher, we all want to do better, we all want to be bigger and better, and we should all be striving to try to do that." The American spirit here is envisaged as personal aspiration and self-improvement. This was echoed in the song she sang to celebrate the opening: "The sky is not the limit, if you dare to spread your wings, conquering new heights." Who knew that making yourself nauseated could be such a noble activity?

Some of the ways Dollywood themes itself around America

are more inclusive than others. Country music has an uneasy and often combative relationship with Hollywood and with California. Usually this is fired by ideological differences between "country values" and those espoused by what Charlie Daniels has called "the Hollywood bunch": "pampered, overpaid, unrealistic children . . . pitiful, hypocritical, idiotic, spoiled mugwumps," as one of his more flattering descriptions puts it. Dolly Parton sets herself up both as an alternative to Hollywood and a proud member of its community, a relationship encapsulated in the witty punning of the name *Dollywood*.

She is also inclusive when it comes to "family values," more so, an incident in July 2011 would suggest, than some of the workers in the park. According to news reports, a woman visiting the park with her wife and the daughters of a friend was wearing a T-shirt bearing the slogan "Marriage Is So Gay." She was asked to turn the T-shirt inside out before she would be allowed to enter. When she asked why, the guard said it was a "family park." Not wanting to create a scene in front of the children, she complied, but after the visit wrote to Dollywood asking for clarification of their policy on dress. PR manager Peter Owens explained: "It doesn't have anything to do with who the people are or what their belief system is. . . . We try to prevent as best we can upon entry of the park one of our guests being offended by something someone else is wearing." Using potential offensiveness as a criterion for a dress code is obviously too subjective; I wonder whether anyone's ever been stopped for wearing a "White Trash" T-shirt that they have purchased at Trinkets and Treasures. But what's important here is the personal statement later issued by Dolly Parton. She explained that the policy about "profanity or controversial messages" on clothing is to protect the individual wearing it as well as to minimize the risk of fights in the park. But she also said the following: "I am truly sorry for any hurt or embarrassment regarding the lesbian and gay T-shirt incident. . . . Everyone knows of my personal support of the lesbian and gay community. Dollywood is a family park and all families are welcome." In 2010 Dollywood won the Applause Award, which Dolly referred to as "the Oscar of the business" presented every other year by Liseberg Amusement Park in Gothenburg, Sweden. Dollywood beat the other nominees, Alton Towers in England and Phantasialand in Germany, in part for its "dedicated leadership honoring family values," as Mats Wedin, the president and CEO of the Liseberg Group phrased it. Even if it has been hard for the theme park always to sustain in practice, Dolly Parton aims not only to honor family values, but also to extend, or even subvert, what that much-touted phrase usually means. It is no surprise that at the first lesbian civil partnership ceremony in England in 2005, the married couple chose to play a Dolly Parton song: "Touch Your Woman."

However, another aspect of Dollywood's Americanism is less inclusive. Dollywood solely and strongly promotes Christianity, the religion that Dolly Parton herself follows. While Tony was taking Athena to clamber on Adventure Mountain, I went into the Liberty store, inspired, said the sales assistant, by Dolly's CD *For God and Country*. The store's merchandise—Stars and Stripes mugs, table cloths, hats and jackets, T-shirts with "US Army" written on them, and Christian art and trinkets—presents an America that is avowedly militaristic and Christian. To love America, suggests the Liberty store, is to love these aspects of America. To leave the store empty-handed, as I did (though tempted by some Stars and Stripes wind chimes), is to risk seeming unpatriotic. Near the Liberty store is Be Attitudes, a store that specializes in Christian merchandise, from "WWJD?" key rings to, ahem, T-shirts with slogans like "Fishers of Men" and "Lifeguard: Mine Walks on Water."

There is also a working chapel in the park, the Robert F. Thomas Chapel (fig. 24). Dr. Thomas was both a physician and a minister, and he worked as the pastor of the chapel until his death in 1981. The current chaplain is a young, slender, and charismatic man who introduced himself to me as Joey Buck. I

24. The Robert F. Thomas Chapel

have since worried I misheard him, as Pastor Buck sounds too
Dickensian a name to be plausible—though in the land of Be
Attitudes anything is possible. He told me that there were two
services on Sundays and that the next service would begin in
fifteen minutes. Was I interested in joining him? I said I didn't
think so, but I was drawn to him and his uncommonly precious
white wood chapel, with its miniature bell and pointed tower
set against a canopy of green trees. I asked him what it was
like being a minister in an amusement park and whether he
was uneasy about a house of God being seen as an "attraction"
(it is listed under "entertainment" and "rides and attractions"
on the Dollywood website). He gave a broad smile and replied
that he is an evangelical Christian and part of his mission is to
draw as many people as he can to Jesus. In an amusement park,
he said, people are more open to new experiences and have

time to try new things. I am sure he is right about visitors' openness; amusement parks take you back to being a child and to having childlike vulnerability. But I find the opportunism of his agenda troubling, even a bit creepy. Having a chapel in an amusement park seems, to this heathen Englishwoman at least, something of a category error.

I did not attend the service, but there was no escaping the sermonizing. Dollywood is the most moralizing place I have been to, beyond the graduation ceremony at my daughter's elementary school. Sententious slogans are everywhere. The sign under the name of the Be Attitudes store could serve as a subtitle for the park itself: "Where Wisdom Is Found." At the exit of Chasing Rainbows we are reminded that "change isn't always bad and it isn't always good, but change is inevitable" and that "paradise is not a goal, but the road itself." A signpost near a bench in a leafy area of the park is a compendium of advice: "Anger is only one letter shorter than Danger," "Start by doing what's necessary, then what's possible, and suddenly you're doing the impossible!" (attributed to St. Francis of Assisi), "Confidence is that cocky feeling you have right before you know better," and "Time is a river without banks."

Moral instruction is part of the theme park tradition. A memorable example is Dreamland on Coney Island, a themed area with a strong moral agenda. It featured an area called Creation whose attractions included the Garden of Eden and Adam and Eve, the End of the World, where sinners got their comeuppance, and Hell's Gate, where you could watch a woman being dragged into the mouth of hell. Dreamland came to an abrupt end in 1911 when it was razed by a fire. In an irony to rival that of the Apollo's Chariot/Fabio's nose incident, but with more catastrophic consequences, the fire started (accidentally) at Hell's Gate. However, the moralizing in Dollywood has more immediate roots, in the influence of Dolly Parton's religious family, especially the sermonizing of her grandfather, who had been a "holy roller" preacher, and the interior of whose chapel is recreated in Chasing Rainbows. It is also an extension of the upbeat New Age aphorizing that has become characteristic of Dolly Parton's persona and songs. Many of Dolly's adages are nudges toward self-improvement: "We cannot direct the wind but we can adjust the sails," "Find out who you are and do it on purpose," "If you don't like the road you're walking on start paving another one." Disneyfication, or Disneyization as it is sometimes called, has come to mean the transformation of society at large into something resembling Walt Disney's theme parks, whether in relation to the promotion of consumption rather than production, or corporate branding, or the theming of urban spaces, like shopping malls. It is a term that is rarely used positively. Dollyfication, if I may coin a phrase, may be the transformation of society at large into an arena for self-improvement.

Of course, Dolly Parton is not responsible for our homiletic culture; there is a fashion for maxims and mottos. Sometimes I feel that I am chided and chivvied throughout the day by inanimate objects. My coffee mug admonishes that "a journey of a thousand miles begins with a single step," and my Philosophy brand shower gel comes with a dissertation on falling in love that opens, "Falling in love doesn't begin with falling in love with others. It begins with falling in love with ourselves. Loving ourselves is healthy and as God intended." I would rather it just made sure that my armpits smell clean. Unlike the life advice on my shampoo and coffee mug, Dolly Parton's comes with wit and is underscored by her personal knowledge of hardship, and recognition that life sometimes sucks. When Dolly sings "Change It," or "Better Get to Livin'," or "Shine Like the Sun," it is hard not to agree. When she tells us there'll be a "Better Day," it seems cynical not to trust her. Living according to the word of Dolly, making a theology, if you like, from her lyrics and mottos, is a scenario dramatized in the novel *How Dolly Parton Saved My Life* by Charlotte Connors. It is an upbeat tale, if a little saccharine, of four Southern women struggling to make a go of a catering business. One of the main characters, Daisy, is inspired to make a better life for herself and her daughter by taking to heart Dolly's aphorisms, such as "If you want the rainbow, you gotta put up with the rain."

So did Dolly Parton save *my* life? Or, to put it another way, was the pilgrimage a success? I thought about this while sitting on a low wall near the chapel and watching the butterflies, the real, sunspot-yellow butterflies, that flitted over the flower gardens along the wide walkways, their bursts of color as vibrant as Dolly Parton's stage costumes. Tony had taken Athena for one last climb on Adventure Mountain. Every pilgrimage is in some ways overdetermined by the generic, as well as the personal, expectations that are projected onto it. The literary tradition of pilgrimage tells us that it is supposed to end with some great moment of revelation, some life-changing epiphany. Like Marcel Proust, the pilgrim seeks "the privileged moment." This is the promise held in the butterfly, Dolly Parton's logo: the promise of metamorphosis and of taking flight. The pressure to have an emotional rags-to-riches experience was so intense that it got in the way of my actually having one.

I had no great epiphany, no moment of wonder akin to our experience of seeing the goddess Athena in the Nashville Parthenon. However, the pilgrimage was a formative experience for me. It was also the catalyst for a more gradual process of change and understanding.

By traveling to Dollywood I had made a connection with a figure who is and has long been important to me, and by whom I entertain the fantasy of being loved. Feeling loved is one of the delusions of being a fan, and it would be a mistake not to recognize it as part of the tacit contractual agreement between idol and admirer, rather than anything to do with me personally. However, it is a pleasant and fortifying idea, and one that Dollywood encourages: *"and above all else love,"* said phantasm Dolly in her attic in Chasing Rainbows, as she brushed off specks of gold from her "life's dust." As I sat on the wall watching the butterflies dance and dart over the flower-beds, hearing the snatches of joyful singing from the chapel, and breathing in smells of leather and caramel, I said a silent thank-you to Dolly Parton. Thank you for sharing your songs, and your special places. Thank you for being a heartening presence, one that stirs me to feel better, do better, and be better.

None of the criticisms that I have of the politics of the Dixie Stampede, or of the rather hackneyed motifs in the presentation of Dolly Parton's biography (as they seem when juxtaposed with similar themes in Loretta Lynn's houses and museum) got in the way of my paying homage to Dolly, a heartfelt homage of genuine gratitude. However, I should now confess that this sensation was totally different not just from my lack of emotion at Graceland, but also from what I had felt a month earlier when I was at the Dolly Parade. After I had seen Dolly on top of her butterfly float I felt disappointed. I was excited to see Dolly Parton in the flesh, to get a glimpse of the real person, but it was nonetheless a sentimental and superficial pleasure, as well as a fleeting one. This had less to do with the spectacle itself than the fact that I had not built up to it, not framed it so that it was invested with emotional importance. I had zipped in and out of Knoxville, without shaking off the everyday concerns of exam grading, laundry, and unpaid bills. In contrast, the physical experience of the pilgrimage to Dolly-wood was crucial to its success. It was necessary to take myself out of my normal environment and routines, to immerse myself in the journey, and to focus on what we were learning about Dolly Parton and her music. This meant that the delight and gratitude I felt in Dollywood seemed earned. It is not that the journey is its own reward, but that the journey affects how you experience the destination.

A more profound realignment concerned my relationship with my new home country, and this has happened more gradually. Throughout my travels across the state I had been confronted with different versions of America and its values.

Dollywood intensified this experience: it has taken elements of America and distilled them into their essences: God, family, patriotic pride, country, nature, memory, and optimism. This dynamic is in the nature of a theme park and is wickedly satirized in Julian Barnes's novel *England, England*. In the novel entrepreneur Sir Jack Pitman proposes to establish an ideal, theme-park version of England on the Isle of Wight. Before building begins, he conducts a survey in twenty-five countries whose results reveal to him the fifty "quintessences of England," the top twenty of which are

1. Royal family
2. Big Ben/Houses of Parliament
3. Manchester United Football Club
4. Class system
5. Pubs
6. A Robin in the Snow
7. Robin Hood and His Merrie Men
8. Cricket
9. White Cliffs of Dover
10. Imperialism
11. Union Jack
12. Snobbery
13. God Save the King/Queen
14. BBC
15. West End
16. Times newspaper
17. Shakespeare
18. Thatched cottages
19. Cup of tea/Devonshire cream tea
20. Stonehenge

Sir Jack discards the less flattering results, including hypocrisy, whingeing, and emotional frigidity (nos. 31, 42, and 46 respectively) as he embarks on creating his destination resort. The list of "quintessences of the USA" extrapolated from Dollywood is both as recognizable and as reductive as those in Sir Jack Pitman's edited catalogue.

However, there was for me a positive repercussion of the theme park's condensation of American symbols and values. Being confronted with an abridged and simplistic image of America, it was hard not to reflect upon what a truer and more realistic representation might be. It would reveal the country's capacity for creativity and innovation, as we saw in the Nashville Parthenon, and musically with the genius of Elvis Presley, and the creative vision of Dolly Parton. It would show the hard-nosed, tell-it-like-it-is side to America, the side that has little truck with sugarcoating and sentimentality, like the blues songs we heard in B. B. King's in Memphis, or in the lyrics to the grittier songs by Loretta Lynn and Dolly Parton. These songs are part of a strong tradition of self-scrutiny and self-criticism (though in Dolly's songs this tends to be limited to a critique of the family rather than national politics). Other countries may criticize America, but the most trenchant voices of dissent have always come from within America itself. Another facet of America is that which we saw embodied in the National Civil Rights Museum: an ability, a need even, to look at one's history in the face, no matter how ugly, and to learn from the mistakes of the past. These are aspects of America that are too gritty for the bland confection of Dollywood. However, it was the park's distillation of, and focus upon, values that prompted me to reconsider mine, and what I respect about America.

The philosopher Richard Rorty has written of relations between people and their country: "You have to describe the country in terms of what you hope it will become, as well as in terms of what you know it to be right now. You have to be loyal to a dream country rather than to the one to which you wake up every morning. Unless such loyalty exists, the ideal has no chance of becoming actual." Through its omissions as well as its attractions, Dollywood helped me see the dream country to which I can be loyal. In that sense, I suppose, I did what Dolly Parton tells us to do in her refrain at Dollywood to "celebrate the dreamer in you."

Of course, the pilgrimage and the process of making sense of it all does not stop once the physical journey ends. Frank Baum must have realized this when he wrote no fewer than thirteen sequels to *The Wonderful Wizard of Oz*. For me, this meant that my journey did not end with the return flight from Knoxville airport (the most twee airport I have ever visited, with wicker rocking chairs instead of molded plastic seats, some adult-sized, some child-sized, lined up in front of the windows). It has continued in the writing of this book. "Eat, Pray, Love, *and Write*" is a more accurate account of what goes into any pilgrimage that is recorded and shared with others. Tony and Athena each have responded differently to their time in Tennessee. Tony says, currying favor, he is pleased to have learned more about Dolly Parton because he knows that she is important to me. He also says that he'll be happy not hearing quite so much about her for a while (though the other day I swear I caught him humming "Two Doors Down"). Athena has moved on from *Hannah Montana* to watching DVDs of *Buffy the Vampire Slayer*, the television series produced by Sandollar Productions, the company co-owned by, and named after, Dolly Parton and her former manager Sandy Gallin. Athena is unimpressed by this association and wants me to write a book about the vampire Spike instead. I still find it strange living in Santa Barbara, where quinoa is considered a food group, and camping a moral imperative. But since my travels in Tennessee, as if the pilgrimage marked a ritual change, and an initiation into America, I have felt much more at home. Now when I look up at the light of a clear blue California morning, I see also, in my mind's eye, the soft heather-hued sky of Dollywood in the Smoky Mountains, and I trust that everything is going to be all right. It's going to be OK.

Doing the Pilgrimage

The best time of year to visit is either early May, when you can make the Dolly Parade the climax to your journey, or in spring or fall when you can avoid the subtropical heat. There are no special preparations to make, but several of the attractions advise you to book a couple of days prior to your visit, so planning ahead is sensible. Dolly Parton's *Dream More* (New York: Putnam Adult, 2012) is essential pilgrimage reading.

GRACELAND

The Graceland ticket office and bus stop (where you get the bus to take you on the tour) is located at 3765 Elvis Presley Boulevard, Memphis, TN 38116. The parking lot is across the street and there is a charge of $10–15. Graceland is open all year round, but its opening hours vary, so it is best to check your precise dates (information and ticket reservations are available online at www.Elvis.com/Graceland or by phone: US or Canada: 1-800-238-2000, International: 1-901-332-3322). The basic tour takes 1–1½ hours and costs $33 for adults, $29.70 for seniors, students, and children 7–12 years old. The Platinum Tour and Elvis Entourage VIP Tour take 2½–3 hours, are more expensive, and allow access to Elvis's airplanes, Automobile Museum, and special exhibits.

From Memphis International Airport head east onto Winchester West, keep on Winchester Road for a mile, and then turn left onto Mill Branch Road, right onto Timothy Drive, and right again onto Elvis Presley Boulevard. Parking will be at the second light on the right. It should take no more than 15 minutes.

HURRICANE MILLS

Loretta Lynn's Ranch is open daily from April to October, and from November to March has more limited opening hours: 9:00 a.m.–4:00 p.m. from Thursday to Monday. It is closed in January and February. Admission is free; there is a small charge for tours, which are offered every hour on the hour.

From Memphis, the journey should take less than 3 hours. Take I-40 East toward Nashville, take exit 143 for TN-13 toward Linden/Waverly, and then turn left onto the Hurricane Mills Road. Follow the signs to the Ranch and Campground, which will be on the right-hand side at 44 Hurricane Mills Road. For further information call 1-931-296-7700 or visit www.LorettaLynnRanch.net. In wet weather it is advisable to wear rain boots, as the ground can get muddy.

NASHVILLE

To drive from Hurricane Mills to Nashville is a largely straight and well signposted route on I-40 East. It takes about an hour and twenty minutes. I know that it is not strictly speaking part of the pilgrimage, but I cannot resist putting in a plug for the Nashville Parthenon. It is in Centennial Park, 2500 W. End Avenue, and is open Tuesday–Saturday, 9:00 a.m.–4:30 p.m., with extended opening hours during the summer.

GRAND OLE OPRY

The Grand Ole Opry and the Gaylord Opryland Hotel have been refurbished and have reopened since my trip to Nashville. For details of shows and backstage tours, and to purchase tickets, go to www.Opry.com or call 1-800-SEE-OPRY. You can get accommodation and concert packages: it is worth checking out at www.GaylordHotels.com/gaylord-opryland/. The concert hall and hotel are next door to one another at 2804 Opryland Drive (the Opry) and 2800 Opryland Drive (the hotel). If you are using a GPS to get there, it is best to use the address 1 Opry Mills Drive. To get there from I-40 East take exit 215 onto the Briley Parkway 155 North, and exit the Parkway at exit 12 (Opryland Hotel). At the time of writing, Gaylord Entertainment and Dolly Parton's Dollywood Company are partnering to develop a "family entertainment zone" (a second Dollywood?) adjacent to the Gaylord Opryland Hotel, anticipated to open in summer 2014.

COUNTRY MUSIC HALL OF FAME AND MUSEUM

Allow around 3 hours to tour the Country Music Hall of Fame and Museum. It has a lovely coffee cart and restaurant, so it can be done in a leisurely way, taking breaks. It is located at 222 5th Avenue South, between 4th and 5th Avenues on Demonbreun Street. Parking is a bit tricky around the museum; discount parking for museum visitors is available at the Pinnacle at Symphony Place Garage at 150 3rd Avenue South (on Demonbreun Street between 2nd and 3rd Avenues). Opening hours are 9:00 a.m.–5:00 p.m. (closed Thanksgiving Day, Christmas Day, and New Year's Day). It is a very popular museum, so it is advisable to book more than 24 hours in advance of your visit (e-mail tickets@CountryMusicHallofFame.org or call 1-615-416-2001). General admission costs $22 for an adult, $20 for seniors, $14 for ages 6–17, free for children aged 5 and under. There are also packages that include a tour of the Historic RCA Studio B. It is worth checking the website ahead of your visit, as they have interesting temporary exhibits.

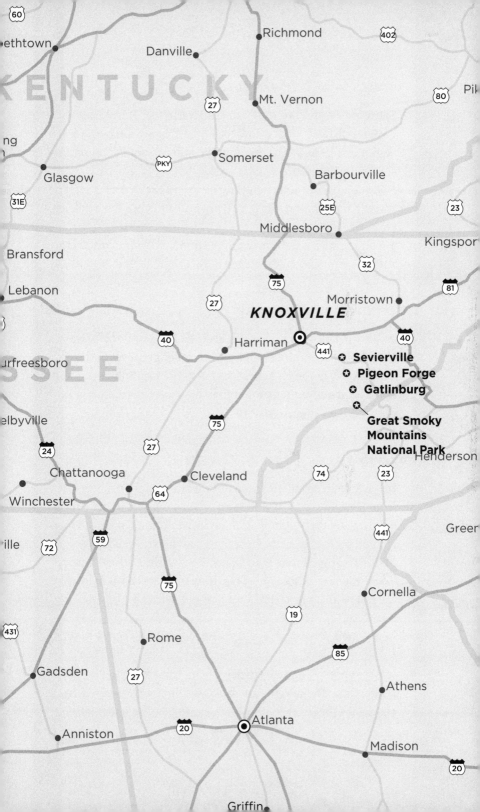

HOMES OF THE STARS TOUR

There are several tour companies in Nashville; Athena and I went with Gray Line, who were very efficient. You need to book ahead at least 2 days before the tour: www.grayline.com/Nashville/Home_of_the_Stars or 615-883-5555. The coach will pick you up from your hotel and drop you back there. Tours run at 9:00 a.m. and 1:30 p.m. daily, and you need to be outside your hotel half an hour prior to those times. The tour takes 3½ hours, with a short break in the middle. Tickets cost $41 for adults, $20.50 for children aged 6–11.

TRINKETS AND TREASURES

At the time of writing, the Trinkets and Treasures store had closed. It has promised to relocate to other premises in the near future. In the meantime, our appetite for Dolly music and books, and occasionally other merchandise, can be satisfied at www.dollyon-line.com/store.

SEVIERVILLE

Driving from Nashville to Sevierville is a straight route east from Nashville on I-40 and takes about 3½ hours. Exit I-40 via exit 407 and turn right onto the Winfield Dunn Parkway. Turn left and you get to Main Street and downtown Sevierville. Main Street intersects with Court Avenue; the Sevier Country Courthouse is located at 125 Court Avenue. It is hard to miss the statue of Dolly Parton on the front lawn.

PIGEON FORGE

It takes about 15 minutes to drive from Sevierville to Pigeon Forge. From the courthouse, head east on Joy Street and turn right onto the Dolly Parton Parkway. The Parkway will take you straight into Pigeon Forge. Alternatively, once you have checked into your hotel in Pigeon Forge or Gatlinburg, it is probably easier to leave the car at the hotel and travel between Sevierville, Gatlinburg, and Pigeon Forge using the Pigeon Forge Trolley. There is a stop at the courthouse. The trolleys are painted green with bears on the side ("Park Your Cares, Ride with the Bears" is their motto), and they run daily from 8:30 a.m. to midnight early March through October, and daily from 10:00 a.m. to 10:00 p.m. in November and December. There are different routes; trolleys running to and from Dollywood run every 15–20 minutes, some others run every 30–45 minutes (for the route maps see www.PigeonForgeTrolley. org). They charge between 50 and 75 cents a trip and are well worth it. With a little advance planning they make it perfectly possible to enjoy the area without a car.

THE DOLLY PARADE

The annual Dolly Parade takes place along the Parkway in Pigeon Forge in early May. Dates are announced on www. PigeonForge.com/Annual-Dolly-Parade. The parade starts at traffic light 6 and ends at traffic light 3. Booking into a hotel along the route so that you can pop back to your room to use the bathroom or grab a coffee was good advice, but if I were to go again I would station myself toward the beginning of the route and not toward the end. You are more likely to see Dolly's superfans, and the children marching in the parade will be less tired.

DIXIE STAMPEDE

The Dixie Stampede is on the Parkway, with a trolley bus stop just outside and a large parking lot. Show times vary according to the season, so it is best to check out the schedule ahead of time: https://Pigeon-Forge.DixieStampede.com/Show_Sched-

1 Graceland

2 National Civil Rights Museum

3 Peabody Hotel

4 Nathan Bedford Forrest Park
(now known as Health Sciences Park)

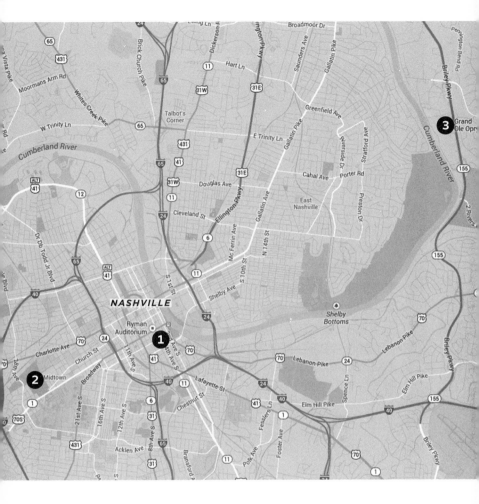

1 Country Music Hall of Fame and Museum
2 Parthenon
3 Grand Ole Opry

ule.php or 1-865-453-4400. If you get there early be sure to check out the horses at the back of the building. Each horse has a sign giving its name and breed, and there are benches where you can sit and watch them being fed and groomed. Dolly Parton songs play over a sound system in the viewing area. Tickets cost between $44.99 and $49.99 depending on where you sit and include the show, dinner, and the Dixie Belle Saloon Opening Act that begins 50 minutes prior to the show. Children age 3 or under are free if they sit on a parent's lap; the amount of stamping the audience is encouraged to do should make a parent think twice about choosing this option.

GATLINBURG

Gatlinburg is a 15-minute drive along the Parkway in the opposite direction to Sevierville. There are signs to the entrance to the Great Smoky Mountain National Park. From the entrance, drive along Cades Cove Loop Road for about 5 miles until you reach the Visitor Center, where you can get directions and advice about hiking and road closures (see also www.nps.gov/grsm). It is worth getting a map before you drive inside the park, because GPS navigation is unreliable. Entrance to the park is free; overnight camping costs $14–$23 per night and advance booking is advisable. The park is open 24 hours a day, 365 days a year, but some roads and facilities close during the winter. Very early morning is the best time to go if you are keen to see the bears.

DOLLYWOOD

You can take the Pigeon Forge Trolley to Dollywood. By car, from the Parkway in Pigeon Forge turn left at traffic light 8 and follow the signs to Dollywood. The park is located at 2700 Dollywood Parks Boulevard, but this is too new an address for most GPS systems; they recognize 1198 McCarter Hollow

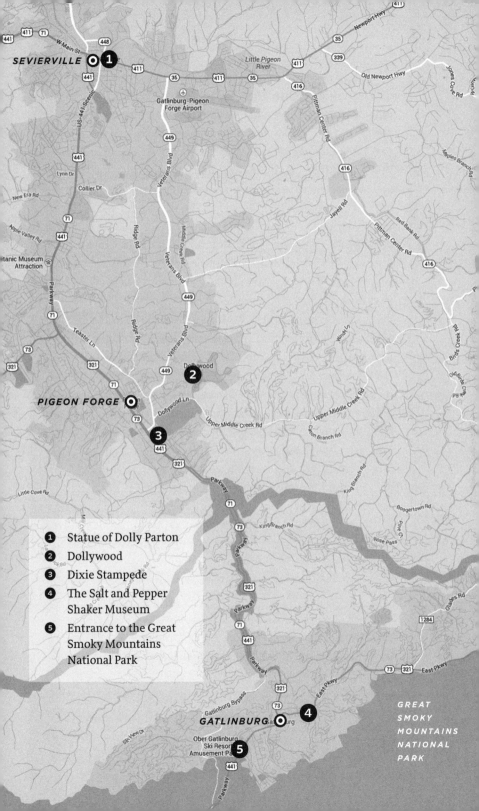

SEVIERVILLE

Little Pigeon River

Gatlinburg-Pigeon Forge Airport

Titanic Museum Attraction

Dollywood

PIGEON FORGE

GATLINBURG

Ober Gatlinburg Ski Resort Amusement Park

GREAT SMOKY MOUNTAINS NATIONAL PARK

1 Statue of Dolly Parton
2 Dollywood
3 Dixie Stampede
4 The Salt and Pepper Shaker Museum
5 Entrance to the Great Smoky Mountains National Park

Road. Dollywood's opening dates and times vary (it is closed for January and February and most of March); a calendar is downloadable from www.dollywood.com, or you can phone their customer service line: 1-800-365-5996. Single-day tickets cost $56 for adults (12–59), $51 for seniors, and $44 for children (4–11). Children 3 and under are free. Season tickets are available, as are passes to Dollywood's Splash Country, the water park next to Dollywood. We did not go to Splash Country, because Athena loves water slides so much we would never have been able to leave and spend time in Dollywood. If you are doing both parks, then consider allowing a few days and getting a season pass ($126 for adults; $114 for children aged 4–11) that allows unlimited park admission. Dollywood also offers accommodation packages with log cabins in Pigeon Forge and Gatlinburg. Despite their whimsical names ("Dream Maker," "Little Lost Bear," "Castle on a Cloud"), log cabins say to Tony and me "Deliverance" and "Straw Dogs," so we chose to stay in a local hotel. However, the cabins make sense for large groups who do not mind self-catering. Dollywood is an exceptionally user-friendly amusement park. For an extra charge ($20 per person) you can rent a Q-bot, a small portable device that will wait in line for you at the most popular shows and rides, although we did not find the crowds oppressive or wait times long. You can rent strollers, wheelchairs, and electric mobility vehicles, and, for dogs, luxurious kennels: Doggywood (of course). If you are very lucky, the people at the entrance turnstiles will smile and say "Miss Dolly will be in the park today."

Further Reading

Because this series does not support the use of notes, I have not been able to make immediate and precise acknowledgment when I have largely drawn on the work of other scholars and quoted from interviews. Quotations from Dolly Parton's lyrics have been taken from the archive of her music at her official website: DollyPartonMusic.net. Her "Dollyisms" are available on Twitter (@Dolly_Parton). An invaluable resource is the newsmagazine www.dollymania.net, which gives regular updates about Dolly Parton and links to fan sites.

Ashdown, Paul, and Edward Caudill. *The Myth of Nathan Bedford Forrest*. Lantham, MD: Rowman and Littlefield, 2005.

Badone, Ellen, and Sharon R. Roseman, eds. *Intersecting Journeys: The Anthropology of Pilgrimage and Tourism*. Urbana: University of Illinois Press, 2004.

Barber, Richard. *Pilgrimages*. Woodbridge, Suffolk: Boydell Press, 1991.

Baudrillard, Jean. *Simulations*. Translated by Paul Foss, Paul Patton, and Philip Beitchman. New York: Semiotext(e), 1983.

———. *America*. Translated by Chris Turner. London: Verso, 1988. Originally published as *Amérique*.

Bender, Amy. *Gatlinburg with the Great Smoky Mountains and Pigeon Forge*. New York: Channel Lake, 2007.

Bradley, Ian. *Pilgrimage: A Spiritual and Cultural Journey*. Oxford: Lion, 2009.

Browning, Jr., Robert M. *Forrest: The Confederacy's Relentless Warrior*. Washington, DC: Brassey's, 2004.

Bufwack, Mary A., and Robert K. Oermann. *Finding Her Voice: Women in Country Music 1800–2000*. Nashville: Country Music Foundation Press and Vanderbilt University Press, 2003.

Caraeff, Ed. *Dolly Close Up / Up Close*. New York: Delilah, 1983.

Ching, Barbara. *"Wrong's What I Do Best": Hard Country Music and Contemporary Culture*. New York: Oxford University Press, 2001.

Cobb, James C. *Redefining Southern Culture: Mind and Identity in the Modern South*. Athens: University of Georgia Press, 1999.

Coleman, Simon, and John Elsner. *Pilgrimage: Past and Present in the World Religions*. Cambridge, MA: Harvard University Press, 1995.

Connors, Charlotte. *How Dolly Parton Saved My Life*. New York: Broadway, 2008.

The Country Music Hall of Fame and Museum: A Pictorial Journey. Nashville: Country Music Foundation Press, 2001.

Cox, Karen L. *Dreaming of Dixie: How the South Was Created in American Popular Culture*. Chapel Hill: University of North Carolina Press, 2011.

Creighton, Wilbur F. *The Parthenon in Nashville: Athens of the South*. Brentwood, TN: J. M. Press, 1989.

Cusic, Don. *Discovering Country Music*. Westport, CT: Praeger, 2008.

Daniels, Charlie. *Ain't No Rag: Freedom, Family, and the Flag*. Washington, DC: Regnery, 2003.

Dickerson, James L. *Go, Girl, Go! The Women's Revolution in Music*. New York: Shirmer Trade Books, 2005.

Dolly Parton and Friends. Orland Park, IL: MPI Media Group, 2007. DVD.

Doss, Erika. "Rock and Roll Pilgrims: Reflections on Ritual, Religiosity, and Race at Graceland." In *Shrines and Pilgrimage in the Modern World*, edited by Peter Jan Margry, 123–142. Amsterdam: Amsterdam University Press, 2008.

Ellison, Curtis W. *Country Music Culture: From Hard Times to Heaven*. Jackson, MS: University Press of Mississippi, 1995.

Elvis Presley's Graceland: Official Guidebook. Memphis: Graceland/ Elvis Presley Enterprises, 2009.

Escott, Colin. *The Grand Ole Opry: The Making of an American Icon*. New York: Center Street, 2006.

Escott, Colin, with Martin Hawkins. *Good Rockin' Tonight: Sun Records and the Birth of Rock 'n' Roll*. New York: St. Martin's Press, 1991.

Fillingim, David. *Redneck Liberation: Country Music as Theology*. Macon, GA: Mercer University Press, 2003.

Fox, Aaron A. *Real Country: Music and Language in Working-Class Culture*. Durham: Duke University Press, 2004.

Fox, Pamela. *Natural Acts: Gender, Race, and Rusticity in Country Music*. Ann Arbor: University of Michigan Press, 2009.

———. "Recycled Trash: Gender and Authenticity in Country Music Autobiography." *American Quarterly* 50.2 (1988): 234–266.

Frith, Simon. "The Academic Elvis." In *Dixie Debates: Perspectives on Southern Culture*, edited by Richard H. King and Helen Taylor, 99–114. New York: New York University Press, 1996.

Garber, Marjorie. *Vested Interests: Cross-Dressing and Cultural Anxiety*. New York: Penguin, 1992.

Gottdiener, Mark. *The Theming of America: American Dreams, Media Fantasies, and Themed Environments*. Boulder, CO: Westport Press, 2001.

Grant, Meg. "How Dolly Does It." In *AARP Magazine*, May–June 2009, 38–41, 63, 72.

Gretlund, Jan Nordby, ed. *The Southern State of Mind*. Columbia: University of South Carolina Press, 1999.

Grobel, Lawrence. "Playboy Interview: Dolly Parton." *Playboy*, October 1978, 81–110.

Gross, Michael Joseph. *Starstruck*. New York: Bloomsbury, 2005.

Guralnik, Peter. *Careless Love: The Unmaking of Elvis Presley*. New York: Back Bay Books, 1999.

Harkins, Anthony. *Hillbilly: A Cultural History of an American Icon.* New York: Oxford University Press, 2004.

Hickey, Dave. "Dolly Triumphant." *Country Music*, July 1974, 25.

"How Dolly Got Rotherham Reading." BBC Radio 4, July 23, 2011, 10:30 a.m.

Inscoe, John C. *Race, War, and Remembrance in the Appalachian South.* Lexington: University Press of Kentucky, 2008.

James, Otis. *Dolly Parton: A Personal Portrait.* New York: Quick Fox, 1978.

Jennings, Dana. *Sing Me Back Home: Love, Death, and Country Music.* New York: Faber and Faber, 2008.

Kingsbury, Paul. *The Grand Ole Opry History of Country Music.* New York: Villard Books, 1995.

Loretta Lynn: The Cinderella Story. Official Guidebook. N.p.: N.d.

Lynn, Loretta, with Patsi Bale Cox. *Still Woman Enough.* New York: Hyperion, 2002.

Lynn, Loretta, with George Vessey. *Coal Miner's Daughter.* New York: Vintage Books, 2010.

Malone, Bill C. *Country Music USA.* Austin: University of Texas Press, 1985.

———. *Don't Get Above Your Raisin': Country Music and the Southern Working Class.* Urbana: University of Illinois Press, 2002.

———. *Singing Cowboys and Musical Mountaineers: Southern Culture and the Roots of Country Music.* Athens: University of Georgia Press, 1993.

Marcus, Greil. *Dead Elvis: A Chronicle of a Cultural Obsession.* Cambridge: Harvard University Press, 1991.

———. *Double Trouble: Bill Clinton and Elvis Presley in a Land of No Alternatives.* New York: Picador, 2000.

———. *Mystery Train: Images of America in Rock 'n' Roll Music.* 5th ed. New York: Plume, 2008.

McCusker, Kristine M. "Sarah Colley Cannon (Minnie Pearl): Gossiping about Grinder's Switch—The Grand Ole Opry and the Modernization of Tennessee." In *Tennessee Women: Their Lives and Times, Volume I*, edited by Sarah Wilkerson Freeman

and Beverly Greene Bond, 261–280. Athens: University of
Georgia Press, 2009.

Miller, Stephen. *Smart Blonde: Dolly Parton; A Biography*. London:
Omnibus Press, 2008.

Morinis, Alan, ed. *Sacred Journeys: The Anthropology of Pilgrimage*.
Westport, CT: Greenwood Press.

Nash, Alanna. *Dolly: The Biography*. New York: Cooper Square
Press, 2002.

———. "Dollywood: A Serious Business." *Ms.*, July 1986, 12–14.

Oermann, Robert K. *Behind the Grand Old Opry Curtain*. New York:
Center Street, 2008.

Ogilbee, Mark, and Jana Reiss. *American Pilgrimage: Sacred
Journeys and Spiritual Destinations*. Brewster, MA: Paraclete
Press, 2006.

The Parthenon: Centennial Park, Nashville, Tennessee. Official
guidebook. N.p.: n.d.

Parton, Dolly. *I Am a Rainbow*. New York: G. P. Putnam's Sons,
2009.

———. *My Life and Other Unfinished Business*. New York:
HarperSpotlight, 1994.

Parton, Dorothy Jo Owens, with Javetta Saunders and Dr. Jerry
Horner. *Dolly's Hero Shares Mighty Mountain Voices*. Dothan,
AL: Royal Reflections, 2007.

Parton, Willadeene. *Smoky Mountain Memories: Stories from the
Hearts of the Parton Family*. Nashville: Rutledge Hill Press,
1996.

Pascoe, Craig S., Karen Trahan Leathem, and Andy Ambrose, eds.
The American South in the Twentieth Century. Athens: University
of Georgia Press, 2005.

Pasternak, Judith Mahoney. *Dolly*. New York: Metro Books, 1998.

Peterson, Richard A. *Creating Country Music: Fabricating
Authenticity*. Chicago: University of Chicago Press, 1997.

Rafter, Nicole Hahn. *White Trash: The Eugenic Family Studies,
1877–1919*. Boston: Northeastern University Press.

Raj, R., and N. D. Morpeth, eds. *Religious Tourism and Pilgrimage*

Management. Wallingford, Oxfordshire: CAB International, 2007.

Reader, Ian, and Tony Walter, eds. *Pilgrimage in Popular Culture*. Basingstoke: Macmillan Press, 1993.

Rinschede, G., and S. M. Bhardwaj, eds. *Pilgrimage in the United States*. Berlin: Dietrich Reimer Verlag, 1990.

Spencer, Brian. *Pilgrim Souvenirs and Secular Badges*. London: Boydell Press with the Museum of London, 2010.

Steinem, Gloria. "Dolly Parton, Musician, Actress, Entrepreneur." *Ms.*, January 1987, 66, 94.

Sternheimer, Karen. *Celebrity Culture and the American Dream*. New York: Routledge, 2011.

Sweeney, Gael. "The King of White Trash Culture: Elvis Presley and the Aesthetics of Excess." In *White Trash: Race and Class in America*, edited by Matt Wray and Annalee Newitz, 249–266. New York: Routledge, 1997.

Tichi, Cecelia. *High Lonesome: The American Culture of Country Music*. Chapel Hill: University of North Carolina Press, 1994.

———, ed. *Reading Country Music: Steel Guitars, Opry Stars, and Honky-Tonk Bars*. Durham: Duke University Press, 1998.

Tosches, Nick. *Country: Living Legends and Dying Metaphors in America's Biggest Music*. London: Secker and Warburg, 1989.

Uhlmann, Tai, director. *For the Love of Dolly*. Los Angeles: Steakhaus Productions, 2008.

Weaver, Bruce J. "What to Do with the Mountain People?": The Darker Side of the Successful Campaign to Establish the Great Smoky Mountains National Park." In *The Symbolic Earth: Discourse and Our Creation of the Environment*, edited by James G. Cantrill and Christine L. Oravec, 151–175. Lexington: University Press of Kentucky, 1996.

Willman, Chris. *Rednecks and Bluenecks: The Politics of Country Music*. New York: New Press, 2005.

Wilson, Benjamin Franklin. *The Parthenon of Pericles and Its Reproduction in America*. Nashville: Parthenon Press, 1937.

Wilson, Gretchen, with Allen Rucker. *Redneck Woman: Stories from*

My Life. New York: Grand Central Publishing, 2006.

Wilson, Pamela. "Mountains of Contradictions: Gender, Class, and Region in the Star Image of Dolly Parton." *South Atlantic Quarterly* 94:1 (Winter 1995): 109–134.

Wolfe, Charles K., and James E. Akenson, eds. *The Women of Country Music: A Reader.* Lexington: University Press of Kentucky, 2003.

Wray, Matt. *Not Quite White: White Trash and the Boundaries of Whiteness.* Durham: Duke University Press, 2006.

Wray, Matt, and Annalee Newitz, eds. *White Trash: Race and Class in America.* New York: Routledge, 1997.

Wright, Chely. *Like Me: Confessions of a Heartland Country Singer.* Milwaukee,WI: Hal Leonard Books, 2011.

ACKNOWLEDGMENTS

Heartfelt thanks to Susan Bielstein, Anthony Burton, Carol Saller, and the readers for the Press, to my colleagues at UCSB, to Hilary McCollum, Sara Lindheim, Rachel Wingfield Schwartz, Margaret Prothero, Noah Segal, Caroline Vout, Sheila Watts, and Sara Castledine, and to my family and fellow travelers Tony and Athena Boyle.